INTRODUCTION

to COMPARATIVE

POLITICS

POLITICAL CONUNDRUMS
AND THE CHANGING WORLD

DR. JACOB DUT CHOL RIAK

The publisher wishes to acknowledge and thank Dr. Douglas H. Johnson for his invaluable help and support for Africa World Books and its mission of preserving and promoting African cultural and literary traditions and history. Dr. Johnson and fellow historians have been instrumental in ensuring that African people remain connected to their past and their identity. Africa World Books is proud to carry on this mission.

Cover design, typesetting and layout: Africa World Books
Unit 3, 57 Frobisher St, Osborne Park, WA 6017
P.O. Box 1106 Osborne Park, WA 6916

DEDICATION

To all the founding fathers of comparative politics; particularly, Harold Laswell, Arend Lijphart, Robert Dahl, Peter Mair and Lee Ray to mention but a few, you have founded a deeply and touching sub-discipline of political science to this changing world. May comparative politics reign forever!

TABLE OF CONTENTS

List of Tables

List of Figures

ACKNOWLEDGEMENT

This book is a result of my 10 years' experience in teaching and research at the University of Juba. My students, both undergraduate and graduate ones have been looking for a reference book for the introduction to comparative politics. Their wishes have come to true with the publication of this book! Indeed, it a great pleasure to appreciate the friends, siblings and colleagues who assisted me to accomplish writing this fourth book in my series of writings. Many thanks to my graduate students in comparative politics who urged and kept reminding me to write this book in comparative politics - as the greatest and the most interesting sub-field of political science. I also offer heartfelt gratitude to Adv. Lual Leek Deng, the founder and managing partner of Visions Law Firm in Juba, for sponsoring the editing of this book. I pay tribute to Africa World Books, particularly, CEO, Peter Lual Reec Deng for publishing it. In a special way, I thank Dr. Sarah Maher, for editing the manuscript.

My appreciation will remain incomplete without giving a special tribute to my dear and beautiful wife, Rechoh Achol Dau Deng aka Achol J. Dut who permitted me to spend time away from her and, our son, Deng as I wrote and completed this fourth book in the series of my book publications. Mama Deng, I am forever grateful for your patience and understanding!

To all those others who assisted me in one way or another in the writing and completion of this book, I am forever grateful to you!

ABOUT THE AUTHOR

The author was born on the 3rd of May 1983 in Malakal, Upper Nile State, in South Sudan. His father is Abraham Chol Riak Akoi, a retired 1st Lieutenant Police Officer, and his mother is the late Daruka Aguet Ajang Duot. Both parents come from Twic East County of Jonglei State. Jacob was conscripted by the SPLA and trained as a child soldier in Dima-Ethiopia military training camp in 1990 and completed his training one year after. He later found his siblings and moved with them to Kapoeta. Within weeks' time, the enemy from the north captured Kapoeta and Jacob with other child soldiers (also known as Red Army) left for Narus at night.

It was in Narus that Jacob commenced his primary school in 1992. When the war raged on in South Sudan, his family moved to Kakuma Refugee Camp, located in the Turkana District of northwestern Kenya. It is there that Jacob completed his Kenyan Certificate of Primary Education (KCPE) in 1998. Having been among the top six best pupils, he won a merit-based scholarship, which was offered by Jesuit Refugee Services (JRS). That scholarship took him to Kakuma Boys High School in 1999. He attended boarding school for four years, subsequently completed secondary education, and sat for the Kenyan Certificate of Secondary Education (KCSE).

In 2003, right after completing high school, Jacob worked with JRS as a Scholarship Desk Officer to give back to the community through community services, especially to thank the Society of Jesus, for being awarded one of their scholarships. In the same year, he engaged as a youth leader in the camp where he offered a lot of help to many fellow refugees through community mobilization, peace education initiatives, inter-community conflict mitigation programs, and women's empowerment. In 2004, he worked with the Lutheran World Federation (LWF) as a primary school teacher and later as an editor of the Kakuma News Bulletin (KANEBU), a refugee-based newsletter.

After all these services to the community, Jacob won another scholarship to study an Advanced Diploma in Social Work and Community Development for two years (2005-2007) at Kobujoi Development Training Institute in Nandi Hills, Eldoret, Kenya. He graduated with a grade of Distinction.

In August 2007, he won another scholarship from JRS to study a BA in Social Sciences with double majors in Political Science and Sociology at the Catholic University of Eastern Africa (CUEA) in Nairobi, Kenya. He later graduated with Summa Cum Laude (First Class Honours) on 1st October 2010 for Degrees in both Sociology and Political Science. While at CUEA, Jacob served as a student leader for both the Sudanese Students' Community and University Guild.

Having appeared in Kenyan newspapers as the Best Student in the Faculty of Arts and Social Sciences in October 2010 graduations, Jacob secured another prestigious scholarship in September 2011 from the Africa Educational Trust (AET) that took him to the London School of Economic and Political Science (LSE) to study a MSc in Comparative Politics at the Department of Government. He graduated in 2012 and returned to South Sudan to commence teaching at the University of Juba where he excelled in research and academic writing. In 2014 he enrolled in a Ph.D. program in Political Science (Comparative Politics) at the University of Juba and graduated in June 2018.

Dr. Jacob Dut Chol Riak is now a respected international comparative political scientist and seasoned senior political analyst who is also an Assistant Professor of International and Comparative Politics and the former Head of Department of Political Science at the University of Juba. He has researched, published and extensively consulted on general comparative politics, comparative hydro politics, comparative democratization, political theory, political parties, ethnic politics, violence and spiritual mythology, peacebuilding, mediations and negotiations, regional integration, particular RECS, secessions and secessionist movements, the politics of petroleum, State building, failure and collapse in Africa, institutional design in divided societies, human rights as well as small arms surveys in South Sudan.

He is a scholar of the Study of US Institutes (SUSI) on American Political Thought. His articles have appeared in international peer-reviewed journals. Dr. Jacob has published several book chapters. He is the author of the three books: *'The Birth of States: Successful and Failed Secessions: A Comparative Analysis of South Sudan, Somaliland and Western Sahara, South Sudan State Formations: Failures, Shocks and Hopes and Regional Integration and South Sudan Accession to the East African Community'*. The three books were published by Africa World Books, Australia in March and July 2021 and September 2022 respectively.

Dr. Riak is a life member of the Development Policy Forum (DPF), Greater Horn Horizon Forum (GHHF), Council for Development of Social Science Research in Africa (CODESRIA), African Peace Building Network (APN), Institute of Security Studies (ISS), Nordic African Institute (NAI), American Political Science Association (APSA) and the International Political Science Association (IPSA) amongst others.

Dr. Riak is the founder and the Executive Director of the Centre for Democracy and International Analysis (CDIA) registered as a research and academic think-tank in Juba. CDIA does policy design and research on good governance and democratization in South Sudan and Africa. He is currently the advisor of South Sudan Accession to Regional Economic Communities (RECs).

ACRONYMS AND ABBREVIATIONS

AET: Africa Educational Trust

BBI: Building Bridges Initiative

CFA Cooperation Framework Agreement

CIA Central Intelligence Agency

CUEA Catholic University of Eastern Africa

CDIA Center for Democracy and International Analysis

DRC Democratic Republic of Congo

EU European Union

FDD Forces for Defense of Democracy

GEMA Gikuyu Embu Meru Association

GERD Grand Ethiopia Renaissance Dam

GWOT Global War on Terror

ICJ International Court of Justice

ICDC Industrial and Commercial
 Development Cooperation

ICTR International Criminal Tribunal for Rwanda

KAMATUSA Kalenjin Maasai Turkana Samburu Association

KANU Kenya African National Union

KCA Kikuyu Central Association

KCPE Kenyan Certificate of Primary Education

KCSE Kenyan Certificate of Secondary Education

KPA Kalenjin Political Alliance

KPU Kenya People's Union

LWF Lutheran World Federation
MENA Middle East and North America
MUF Mwambao Union Front
NBI Nile Basin Initiative
OECD Organization for Economic Cooperation
 and Development
RECS Regional Economic Communities
RPF Rwanda Patriotic Front
SPSS Statistical Programme for Social Scientists
SUSI Study of United States Institutes
THA Taifa Hills Association
UN United Nations
UMA Ukambani Members Association
UNESCO United Nations Educational Scientific and
 Cultural Organization
WHO World Health Organization
YKA Young Kavirondo Association

CHAPTER ONE

1.1 Definitions, Scope and Nature of Comparative Politics

Comparative Politics is a sub-field of Political Science. Public Administration, Political Theory, International Relations, International Law, Public Policy Analysis, Political Economy, Political Sociology and Political Psychiatry are also sub-fields of Political Science. The study of Comparative Politics essentially enables us to understand the diversity of processes and institutions of states across the ages and periods. When we look at the politics, economics and institutions of the various states of the world we discover that there exist wide variations and conundrums which raises the questions of 'why' did such variations and conundrums arise? The *general* questions are:

- Why are some countries poor and others wealthier?
- What enables some countries to 'make it' in the modern world while others remain perpetually poor?
- Why do poor countries often find themselves under authoritarian regimes, while the richest countries are democratically governed?
- Why are some countries torn by ethnic violence while others have ethnic peace?
- Why did states that inherited parliamentary systems change to a presidential system?
- What are the internal social and political conditions as well as the

international structures of these various countries that explain the similarities as well as the differences?

- Why the emergence of Comparative Hydropolitics?
- Why the political transformation of the world politics?

The above questions are critical and shall be answered in this book.

Besides, comparative politics asks *casual* questions of *why* and *how* did things turn out the way they did? Besides, comparative politics asks questions about political *'outcomes'* within nation-states.

1. What kinds of answers do comparative politics scholars see as valuable?

- A valuable explanation of political outcome relies on arguments that are at least potentially relevant in more than one case (in other words, a good answer has *"comparative significance"*)

2. How do comparative politics scholars justify their conclusions scientifically?

- In lots of distinct ways. One way is through drawing conclusions using qualitative inferences. Another way is drawing conclusions using quantitative inferences.

It is important to note that a core conviction behind the design and application of comparative politics is that "if once can't participate in the argument about scientific standards, one can't take advantage of what comparative politics has to offer" (Chol, 2012). Scientific standards include the use comparative method, surveys, case studies, process tracing and regression analysis to showcase comparative politics and governance.

According to Lee Ray (2004), the study of government is the beginning point of comparative politics (Ray, 2004). While the structures and behaviors of governments, as Ray (2004) argues, constitute an existing and challenging area of concern for students of comparative political science, modern governments are hitherto emerging more and more as indispensable instrumentalities of multifaceted development and also as an active force in the forming of economic, social and environmental conditions. This is especially in the developing region of Asia, Africa, and Latin America, and also as an active force in the forming of economic, social and environmental conditions. Globally, there are varieties of political systems that represent the governments and the politics we have in the world today. Some of these political systems are very ancient, meaning that they are very old in creation. These ancient political systems include sultanic and feudal lords' structures. Some political systems are modern in the discourse of social sciences and more akin political science. These modern political systems include liberal and representative democracies and good governance. These different political systems have captured an enormous variety of institutions, processes, and interactions in both the private and public spheres. Thus, it is extremely difficult to see two countries that are completely identical without any slightly different in their formations and structures. In other words, governments have varied complexity in their functionalities and delivery of services.

Hence, comparative politics involves the systematic study and comparison of the world's political systems. It seeks to explain differences between as well as similarities among countries and themes. In contrast to journalistic reporting on a single country, comparative politics is particularly interested in exploring patterns, procedures, processes and regularities among political systems and the states. It looks for trends, changes in patterns and processes and procedures. Its tries to develop general propositions or hypothesis that describe and explain these trends. It seeks to do such comparisons rigorously and systematically, without grinding personal, partisan, or ideological axes. Comparative politics involves hard work, clear thinking, impartial discussions, careful and thorough scholarship, and above all, clear, consistent, and balanced writing.

On other hands, Thomas Magstadt and Peter Schotten (1999) in their seminal book *"Understanding Politics, Ideas, Institutions and Issues"* show how Comparative Politics helps to formulate meaningful generalizations about government and politics across countries and the states (Magstadt and Schotten, 1999). Some comparative political scientists have specialized studying a particular state and political systems intensively. Others political scientists focus their attention on a particular political phenomenon such as instability or voting behavior in the polity. As argued earlier, comparative politics compare systems of government in the global states. For example, a comparative political scientist might investigate the impact of political parties' activities on elections in United Kingdom, Australia or United States of America.

To Michael Sodaro (2007), comparative politics is simply an examination of political realities in countries all over the world, looking at the many ways people behave in politics (Sodaro, 2007). It also examines political activities within individual countries, and then compares with the domestic experiences of others. For instance, we can compare various democracies with one another to learn more the process of democracy and its critiques. We can as well compare various non-democratic governments to learn more about how they work. For example, the communist countries or military dictatorships states. Besides, Gregory Marter (2001) asserts that some people view comparative politics from the angle of relativity, in terms of bigger, stronger, freer, more stable, less democratic, and so on (Marter, 2001). Comparative politics, then, involves no more and no less than a search for similarities and differences between and among political phenomenon, these including political institutions (such as legislatures, political parties, or political interest groups), political behavior (such as voting, demonstrating, or reading political pamphlets) or political ideas (such as liberalism, conservatism, or Marxism). The central view political science as the master science also constitutes the thrust of comparative politics and its deity. On the whole, comparative politics is characterized by an empirical approach based on the comparative method.

Arend Lijphart (2010) argues that comparative politics does not have a *substantive* focus in itself, but rather a methodological one: it focuses on "the *how* but does not specify *what* of the analysis" (Lijphart, 2010). In other words, the object of its study does not define comparative politics, but rather by the method it applies to study political phenomena and events. Peter Mair and Richard Rose (2010) advanced a slightly different definition, arguing that comparative politics is defined by a combination of a substantive focus on the study of countries' political systems and a method of identifying and explaining similarities and differences between these countries using common concepts (Mair and Rose, 2010). In nutshell, comparative politics has therefore entailed the study of different political institutions, processes and structures as they interact in a given polity or polities.

The nature of comparative politics is that it has emerged as an important tool in the analysis of political systems and their changes in the troubled world. To compare basically means to look for similarities and differences, to look for good features and bad features and to look for things that seem to work and those that do not. According to French social philosopher, Alexis De' Tocqueville (1962) "comparison is fundamental to all human thoughts and it is the mythological core of the scientific method" (Tocqueville, 1962). This therefore means that we cannot be scientific in social sciences if we are not comparing and this is mainly due to the nature of social science discipline where laboratory experiments are conducted as they are in other social sciences. Thus, the best that can be done is to compare phenomenon or events that takes place in different political environments in a polity.

An important distinctive feature of comparative politics is its emphasis on states and nations, which are compared in their various characteristics and in most cases, the comparative method is used to study states with identical political structures. Such structures include political systems, institutional arrangements and historical formation of the states. The main reasoning behind comparative politics is the belief that one can better understand the political process and performances of countries if one compares the political system of different countries.

Overall, comparative politics is a sub-field of political science that asks casual questions about political outcomes within nation-states, seeking answers of comparative significance while arguing scientific standards.

1.2 Why Study Comparative Politics?

Comparative politics is not only intellectually stimulating, it also helps to achieve the following objectives:

i.   To capture and analyze the major political similarities and differences between countries.

ii. To develop perspectives on the mixture of countries and variability, which characterizes the world's governments and the political contexts in which they operate.

iii. To enable us to understand how nations change and the patterns that exist within those changes. These changes and patterns are critical for forestalling the world to come.

iv. To help scholars to overcome false world. There are a lot of falsehoods in the world about the future of comparative politics. These falsehoods include the failure and extinction of comparative politics amongst the social sciences of the world. Some of these falsehoods can be overcome when scholars compare to get the best.

v.   To encourage intellectual stimulating. Intellectualism is a cornerstone in our advancement and scientific analysis.

vi. To employ rigorous, eclectic and effective methodologies in a commitment to show that the study of politics is scientific.

CHAPTER TWO

2.1 Theories of Comparative Politics

A theory is a set of propositions and/or hypotheses that are logically related to each other (Coplan, 1971). Theory brings organization and the capacity to accumulate knowledge to a field and it enables scholars to tie together the propositions they have developed at different levels and at different time. Hence, in political science and in particular in comparative politics, a theory is used primarily to explain political facts and predictions. Theory may also be referred to as a set or a system of statements logically interconnected in various complexes.

While Daniel Coplan (1971) pioneered the definition of a theory, other comparative political scientists have defined it too. According to Arthur Kalleberg (1983), a theory is a system of interrelated definitions and empirically interpreted hypotheses (Kalleberg, 1983). In the opinion of James Price (2003), a theory consists of propositions, concepts, assumptions and scope of conditions (Price, 2003). Propositions, as Price further observes, are the core of a theory and are viewed as statements of causal relations between two or more concepts. Indeed, a theory is characterized by multiple propositions. Moreover, Arthur Kalleberg (1983) has however criticized what social action theorists mean by theory, saying it is more of a "frame of reference" rather than a theory itself (Kalleberg, 1983). Social action theorists define theory as a framework of social interactions in a society. The criticism of theory with regard to social action equally extends to political science and in particular, comparative politics because comparative political scientists more or less study political action as other social science disciplines do, especially sociology. In view of the above therefore, what is needed is a set of hypotheses expressed in a tangible form and a series of verifying studies designed to test those set of hypotheses. Hence, three theories of comparative politics are discussed below:

2.2 General Systems Theory

It is with no doubt that the emergence of the behavioral approach has translated comparative politics into a change of both analytical tools and methodological framework from what it used to be under the traditional or ancient model. Behavioral approach articulates the interactions of systems in a society. These interactions are dictated by the human behaviors. The traditional approach is tweaked on the inter-actions of ecosystem in a society. The new methodological approach is argued on the interactions of human beings and environment in a system and it has equipped students of government and politics with the required analytical tools, conceptual frameworks and models within which critical evaluation of political phenomena may be executed. The new methodological approach places more emphasis on empiricism rather than normative study. Consequently, a number of theories have been developed under the scholarly ambit of behavior to empirically study and explain political phenomena in a comparative world. In the view of Roy Macridis (2004), the most important thing in general systems theory is a number of system approaches which are drawn from the general systems theory itself (Macrisdis, 2004). Historically, systems theory had its root in natural science. However, the theory was the result of the movement aimed at the unification of science and above all, the scientific analysis.

It was the intention of the proponents of the systems theory to find a central point that could serve as a wider platform for creative and critical analysis. The intensification of efforts toward this direction, particularly, after the Second World War, crystallized around the concept of systems, which Von Bertalanffy (1968), the German biologist, defined as a set of "elements standing in interaction" (Bertalanffy, 1968). The concept is predicated on the notion that objects or elements within a group are not only related in one way or the other, but also, in turn, interact with one another on the basis of certain identifiable processes. The utility of systems theory is most relevant in political analysis because it not only identifies the components in any framework or social system but also encourages the evaluation of the patterns and levels of relationships among different units. It therefore establishes the fact of interrelatedness and interdependence of distinct but within the interactional units.

Although systems theory has its origin in the natural sciences, it was adopted and adapted as an analytical framework in political science, particularly, comparative politics in the middle of the twenty centuries. For instance, David Easton (1953), one of the major pioneers of the application of systems theory to political studies, defines a political system as "behavior or set of interactions through which authoritative allocations (or binding decisions) are made and implemented for society" (Easton, 1953). To be sure, a system is marked by different actions and integrations.

The proponents of the system theory identify three primary components of every political system. These components include the political community; the regime; and the authorities. By this, the political community comprises of people who are bound together by a political division of labor. The regime in this case includes the constitutional legal structures as well as the political processes for institutional norms. Those individuals who exercise power as the agents of the state at any given time constitute the political authorities. The general systems theory operates with certain basic concepts: the first among the concepts, is descriptive concept. This includes, for instance, open and closed systems, organismic and non-organismic systems, hierarchical levels as subsystems, and orders of interaction and scale effect. Also important are concepts of general systems theory that deal with the factors for the regulation and maintenance of systems. In this taxonomy are concepts like stability and equilibrium among others. Other concepts include boundaries, input and output specifically relating to aspects of organization. Some concepts also pay attention to the dynamic of change, capturing both disruptive and non-disruptive notions of adaptation. Some of these concepts enable us to understand why a system may break down and some while others thrive. They may also highlight under what condition a system comes under stress due to overloading and inappropriate set up of the system. Indeed, there are myriads of concepts that the students of comparative politics could take advantage of in understanding factors that facilitate political stability and those that are a threat to the stability of a polity. This perhaps explains why Roy Macridis (2004) notes that the general systems theory provides a broad framework for the examination of politics (Macridis, 2004).

Offshoots of the Systems Theory

To develop new methods for the purpose of political analysis, some basic frameworks and terminologies of the general systems theory have to be adapted by the behavioralist. David Easton (1953) has been credited with developing an original and unique systemic approach for the purpose of political analysis (Easton, 1953). Easton developed the input-output analytical framework. This model stresses the behavior of the political system vis a vis that of its environment in terms of analyzing inputs (demands as supports) and outputs (authoritative allocation of values or policy decisions and actions). Easton intended to make his theory an all-purpose theory that is capable of being utilized to analyze any form of political systems or international political system. In fact,

David Easton (1953) sees a political system as a system of interaction in any society through which binding or authoritative allocations are made and implemented. Thus, wherever authoritative decisions are made the input-output functions are performed, either at the local or international political levels.

Weakness of the Easton Input – Output Approach

The input-output analytical framework has proven useful and remains an excellent technique for comparative political analysis. This is more so because it is focused on an overview of entire political systems and has an inclusive set of concepts and categories which facilitate comparison. As useful and comprehensive as the input-output approach is, it has certain glaring weaknesses. These include, the presumptions that questions concerning system persistence as the most important and inclusive subjects for political analysis may not be always tenable.

It is also essential to note that despite the importance of the analytical framework, contrary to the expectations of Easton, the input-output theory falls short of being a general theory of politics in the real sense of the word. Thus, such a focus may be fruitful, but does not result in a general 'theory' of politics. The theory is narrow with a highly restricted coverage with regard to the interactions among the different political systems. Finally, the theory, which focuses on the politically active and relevant members of society, tends to give it an elitist orientation.

2.3 Structural Functional Theory

The structural functional theory is one of the foremost system-derivatives in political science, and a major framework for comparative political science research. According to Bernard Sussie (1992), in practical sense, structural-functionalism often presupposes a 'system' view of the political world that is uncertain (Sussie, 1992). Although structural functionalism originated from anthropology and has been applied in sociology, it has been adopted as a framework for political analysis in political science. Indeed, it was adopted in the field of comparative politics by Gabriel Almond. According to Gabriel Almond (2017), this mode of analysis is fundamentally concerned with the phenomena of system maintenance and regulation (Almond, 2017). The basic theoretical proposition is that in all social systems, certain basic functions have to be performed. The central question is: 'what structure can fulfill basic functions and under what conditions in any way given system? In the words of Radcliff Brown (1990), function is the contribution that a partial activity makes to the total activity of which it is a part (Brown, 1990). The function of a particular social usage is the contribution it makes to the total political system.

The theory presupposes that a political system is often made up of several structures which are "patterns of action and resultant institutions" (Brown, 1990). While there are different institutions and patterns of actions, they all however have certain functions which are defined as 'objective consequences for the system. By this, a function is, therefore, a regularly recurring pattern of action and behavior carried in for the preservation and advancement of the system. Although various institutions perform different functions, a system may sometimes become dysfunctional. The reverse of function is in fact dysfunctional. Dysfunctional implies an action detrimental to the existence of growth of the system. A certain degree of dysfunction is inevitable in the operation of any pattern of action on occasion, it is possible to identify actions or decisions which are functional for the political system as a whole for some of its components but dysfunction for certain groups or individuals. On the other hand, structures refer to those arrangements within the system which perform the functions. According to Gabriel Almond (1990), there is no such thing as a society which maintains internal and external order which has no 'political structure and political vision' (Almond, 1990). Robert Merton (1981) contends that a given function can be fulfilled by many different structural political arrangements (Merton, 1981).

Gabriel Almond (1990) then developed a list of functional requisites and divided them into four inputs and three output functions. The four functions are: political socialization & recruitment, interest-articulation, interest-aggregation, and political communication. The three output functions, performed by nongovernmental systems, by society, and the general environment, are regarded as highly significant (Almond, 1990). Also, the output functions are performed by traditional government agencies like the legislature, the executive, the judiciary and the bureaucracy.

2.4 Modernization Theory

This theory was influenced by the writing of Karl Marx, Emile Durkheim and Max Weber. These thinkers were further influenced by the writings of Talcott Parsons. It was the main comparative political science theory during the 1950s and 1960s. It assumes that modernization is a linear, inevitable process and that compares countries in the Global South to countries in the Global North based on their level of modernization. It argues the importance of leveled-field advancement in socio-economic and political spheres, particularly, political institutions and systems. Modernization theory is criticized for being western-centric, it assumes the level of modernization of countries in the Global North to be the universal ideal. It also minimizes or excludes the impacts of history, culture and religion on the different levels of development between countries.

The theory looks at the internal factors of a country while assuming that with strong support, traditional or under developing countries can be brought to development in the same manner more developed countries have been. Modernization theory both attempts to identify the social variables that contribute to political, social change and development of societies and seeks to explain the process of political, economic, social progress and evolution. Authors such as Daniel Lerner (1968) and others have explicitly equated modernization with westernization (Lerner, 1968).

The Global North and the Global South are terms to differentiate between countries (mostly) in the northern hemisphere characterized by richer economies, such as the USA, Western Europe, Japan and Australia; and countries (mostly) in the southern hemisphere, with poorer economies, most of which were former colonies of the great powers and are found in Southeast Asia and Sub-Saharan Africa.

CHAPTER THREE

After the definition of comparative politics in chapter one, theories of comparative politics in chapter two, it becomes necessary to discuss forms of comparison. These forms of comparison are discussed as below:

3.1 Forms of Comparison

There are range of comparisons forms that scholars of comparative politics may undertake from time to time:

i. **Studies of one country**. This includes a particular institution (political parties, militaries, parliaments, interest groups), political process (decision making), or public policy (for instance, labor or welfare policy) in that country.

ii. **Studies of two or more countries**. These comparative studies are harder to carry out, and they are usually more expensive in terms of travel and research cost. Hence, the studies of comparative politics do a case study of one country first and later move on to study others and elaborate the comparison between them. Such a step is very important intellectually because it is in knowing and writing about two or more countries that students can begin to make genuine comparisons.

iii. **Sub-regional or area studies.** These may include studies of Africa, Latin America, the Middle East, East Asia, South East Asia, Europe or other sub regions (Southern Europe or North Africa for example). Such studies are useful because they involve groups of countries that may have several things in common – for example, similar histories, cultures, languages, geographic locations, legal systems, religions, colonial backgrounds, and so on.

iv.   **Studies across regions**. These studies are becoming more prevalent, but at more advanced levels, they are often expensive and difficult to carry out. One must know, master and travel to not just one region but to two or more regions. Such studies might involve for example, comparisons of the role of the military in Africa and the Middle East or of the quite different paths to development of the East Asian countries and Latin America.

v.   **Global comparisons.** With the improved statistical data collected by the World Bank, the UN, and other agencies, it is now possible to do comparison on global basis. Such studies can best be done through the use of statistical correlation tools such as SPSS or STATA. But such correlations cannot be said to prove causation, for instance, economic growth causes democratization, there is a relationship between economic growth and democracy, but the first does not necessarily cause the second.

vi. **Thematic studies.** Comparative politics focuses on themes as well as countries and regions as argued earlier. For example, some scholars may be interested in the changing role of the state in a comparative perspective, in the process of military professionalization as seen comparatively, in the structure of class relations as analyzed comparatively, or in the process of political socialization. Others may be interested in such themes as dependency theory (the dependence of some countries on others), the process by which emerging countries achieve national development, or the newer systems of interest group representation called "corporatism" viewed from a comparative viewpoint.

After discussion of the forms of comparison, it is necessary to discuss the merits and demerits of the comparative method.

CHAPTER FOUR

4.1. Merits and Demerits of the Comparative Method

After the discussion of forms of comparison in chapter three, an analysis of merits and demerits of the comparative method is very necessary. Below is the discussion:

4.2. Merits of Comparative Method

i.   The main justification for engaging in a comparative study of politics is related to the basic nature of social sciences where it is impossible to make use of experimental methods of research. The political scientist unlike the physical scientist for example, cannot conduct precise experiments in order to determine for instance the degree to which a leader influence the policy outcomes in a country.

ii. The comparative method also supplies meaningful contrast, without which no explanation is possible. Thus, comparative politics may allow for the testing of intermediate steps in argument.

iii. Comparative method also helps us to avoid what is called ethnocentrism, which means that we are able to avoid the temptation to a false universe, which was quite common in most of the traditional studies of political systems. At that time, it was assumed by authors that a theory developed in one country could be applied universally to all countries. Scholars during that time generated theories that they considered to be generally applicable to all countries without considering the fact that different countries have their own peculiar and unique ways of managing their own affairs, depending on their historical and environmental contexts.

iv. The comparative method enables us to develop theories, hypotheses and concepts. The hypotheses for example try to relate two or more variables/factors and can suggest, for instance, a relationship between electoral and party systems of governments or the relationship between war and revolution in a polity.

v. The comparative method helps in improving classifications. Classification is considered to be a stepping-stone in the journey toward explaining events. For example. once we have managed to classify executives into presidential and parliamentary types then we are able to investigate the various factors that determine that the effectiveness of various systems of government. Without variation and some kind of classification, we would not be able to explain anything.

vi. Comparative method enables us to make predictions. Prediction follows after generalization. For example, if we know that electorates prefer high unemployment to high inflations control policies then we can be able to appropriately advise the government to pay maximum attention to high unemployment condition in the country by providing jobs opportunities. It can be predicted in this case that anti-inflation policies are more likely to enable the government to win any re-election than a full employment policy; and

vii. Comparative method helps us to see a wider range of political alternatives and illuminates the virtues and short-coming in our own political life by taking us out of the network of assumption and familiar arrangements within which we usually operate. Comparative method helps us to expand our awareness of the possibilities of politics thus when we compare the past with our present of our political systems and compare our own political systems with that of other States. This can help us to deepen our own understanding of our institutions.

Demerits of Comparative Method

i. How to weigh detail against generalizability. Academics and researchers are advised to take a lot of care when choosing how many cases they examine and they should try to weigh how much detail they give and how much generalization they make. Thus, comparative method runs a risk of either giving too much detail on one hand or generalizing too much on the other hand;

ii. Presence of too many variables. When we use the comparative method, we find that there are too many variables, all of which cannot be adequately treated. Very rarely will one find that one country is totally similar to another country in such a way that we can have a tightly controlled comparison or experiments. This therefore, makes a comparison to be quite difficult because a number of factors have to be considered for each country or case;

iii. There is a problem of bias. Bias is regarded as one of the main problems of comparative method. In this case, bias means the values of a researcher or an analyst will determine or affect the results of the study and therefore such studies may not yield accurate results; and

iv. Extensive knowledge requirement: Comparison is only contemplated when more than one country is involved. A comparative study involves at least two countries and could include many more. A statistical comparative analysis, could examine the relationship between democracy and economic development, and might draw information from all the countries of the world. Clearly, comparative political studies can be substantial.

CHAPTER FIVE

5.1. Historical Origin and Different Phases of Development of Comparative Politics

a) The Historical Origin

The attempt to study politics comparatively started as early as about 2000AD. Philosophers like Aristotle, Plato, and Socrates among others blazed the trail in this regard. In his book *'Politics'*, Aristotle contrasts the economies and social structures of many Greeks city states in an effort to determine how social and economic environments affected the political institutions and policies of those political systems. Plato then emphasized comparatively the importance of Republics in his groundbreaking book *'The Republics'* to common men in order to advance human progress through governments. From then on, other scholars have made attempts to engage in comparative studies of different political systems. For example, a modern political scientist, Robert Dahl (1989) in his study of democracy, compares the economic characteristics, cultures and historical experiences of different countries in order to discover the combination of conditions and characteristics that are associated with various forms of governments (Dahl, 1989). However, it is necessary to point out that any attempts to study institutions comparatively actually predate the era of traditional philosophers mentioned above. For instance, several chapters of the Bible include several comparisons of Israel with other states around them. God, according to the Bible, constantly compared Israel with other nations each time the Israelites took a wrong step, or when they sinned against Him. God compared the state of Israel and its governance with the states of the gentiles to see in what ways the Israelites had conformed to the lifestyle of the states around them.

b) Different Phases of Development of Comparative Politics

i. The Traditional Phase

The traditional epoch was essentially the era of philosophers like Aristotle, Plato and Socrates who focused on the institutions of government. Essentially, the philosophers who belong to that epoch studied the institutions of government by way of describing how they operated. Their analysis was predicated on the constitutional basis of the working of the institutions of government. They studied political institutions to discover what state is best governed and what form of government best served the common good. Aristotle compared existing political systems in order to theorize about the best possible regime as his ultimate concerns were ethical in nature and he was interested in questions of justice. Aristotle studied 50 Greek city states and categorized them into different system of governments (Aristotle, 1888). His empirical investigations were driven by such questions as:

- What is the good life?
- What form of government is best?
- What is the relationship between the type of political regime in a given place and the moral character of the people who live under them?

ii. The Renaissance Phase

This is the era of the rebirth or revival of comparative politics in Europe. Philosophers like John Locke, Thomas Hobbes and John Montesquieu and Niccolo Machiavelli were some of the major actors during this renaissance phase. Essentially, these philosophers, among others, focused on the institutions of government by studying the workings of the institutions of the various European states. They were highly normative in their study. Thus, they were concerned with how best a state should be organized such as:

- What should be the basis of authority that will command obedience from the citizens?
- Should citizens obey government and what form of government is best for the society?

The philosophers who belong to this epoch, like the traditionalists before them, were basically prescriptive in approach. That is because they merely studied institutions comparatively to explain a form of government as either bad or good and often accounted for the reasons for the observable development in the institutions.

iii. The Age of Enlightenment

The third epoch in comparative politics is the age of enlightenment. The 18th-century intellectual movement in Western Europe emphasized reason and science in philosophy and in the study of human culture and the natural world. This phase included philosophers like David Richardo, Adams Smith, Karl Marx, Fredrich Engel, Nigel among others. During the historical phase, the philosophers made efforts to elevate intellectual activity to the realm of scientism. Beyond the level of common sense and reason, the philosophers started to provide explanations to justify the political, social, and economic structure and system of their time. For instance, Karl Marx studied the origin of modern states through human history using the scientific method. He succeeded in describing the various phases in human history. According to him, these phases included communalism, slavery, feudalism, capitalism, socialism and communism.

However, as evident in the work of Karl Marx, the approach of this epoch is equally prescriptive. Nevertheless, the thinking of these scholars has largely shaped the world's political system and processes. For instance, the Russian revolution of 1917 pioneered by Joseph Lenin, an apostle of Marx, was to give effect to Marx's idea on socialism. Also, Adams Smith's theory on international trade with regard to comparative and absolute advantage in world trade is still as valid as ever.

iv. The Modern Era

In the modern epoch, emphasis has shifted from mere focusing on the institutions of government to a critical examination of the processes and activities of both actors and institutions, as well as the behavior of institutions using scientific procedures. Basically, this era succeeded in taking political studies out of the traditional and description domain by adopting scientific tools in the study of politics. Scholars who belong to this epoch include David Easton, Robert Dahl, Gabriel Almond, Harold Lasswell, Arend Lijphart, Arthur Kalleberg and others. These scholars attempt to study politics comparatively by gathering and analyzing data, so as to provide an explanation for certain political development, the ultimate aim of which is to be able predict political phenomena. In this epoch, scholars wish to establish the relationship between A and B or C and D, and if there is no relationship, then the probable reason for the absence of a relationship.

CHAPTER SIX

6.1 Approaches to Study of Comparative Politics

There are fundamentally two approaches to the study of comparative politics. They include the traditional approach and the institutional approach.

a) The Traditional Approach

The traditional approach became popular among many American political scientists in the 19th and early 20th centuries and has up to date continued to attract consideration in political discourse. According to Lee Ray (2000), "the traditional approach to the study of comparative government grew out of a response to the historicism of the nineteen centuries" (Ray, 2000). The approach placed much emphasis on the formal and legal aspects, as well as the political institutions of the states in its analysis. The approach embraces the descriptive method in explaining any political phenomenon. The most important ones are the historical, legalistic and institutional approaches.

Right from its inception in the 19th century, US Political Science was looked upon by many of its practitioners as primarily a historical discipline. In the opinion of the people, only a thin line of separation was thought to lie between history and political science. Political science was even considered a branch or division of the former. Richard Jensen (1984), who avers that the motto of the generation of political scientists was "history is past politics and politics present history" (Jensen, 1984) underscores this. In other words, political science was seen primarily as political history; and included such fields as the history of political parties, foreign relations and great political ideas.

Furthermore, it appears and in fact always seemed natural to limit the study of politics to law or legal system. This is the legalistic perspective of the study of politics. This approach, which has its origin among US political scientists, conceives political science primarily from the standpoints of studying constitutions and legal codes. Those who study politics from this perspective endeavor to answer questions relating to politics and actions of political actors from the constitutional or legal underpinning of actions.

Characteristics of the Traditional Approach

The traditional approach to the study of comparative government is essentially non-comparative. Most studies in the area of comparative government deal either with one country or with parallel descriptions of the institutions of a number of countries. An overwhelming proportion of literature in this field illustrates this fact. This schools the students of comparative government in constitutional foundations, the organization of political power as well as a description of the ways in which such powers are exercised in each case.

Another characteristic of the traditional method is that it is descriptive in approach. One of the major characteristics of the traditional approach is that it adopts the historical method, while the work was largely legalistic. It was therefore highly descriptive. Consequently, we may contend that undertaking the description of the formal political institutions is vital for the understanding of the political process and that as such leads to comparative study. A great proportion of the study carried out with the utility of the traditional approach often carries out separate descriptions of the institutions of individual countries and fails to make explicit comparisons. In most cases, the works describe various political institutions generally without attempting to compare them. Consequently, only a very negligible comparison is done in reality. And this is in fact limited exclusively to the identification of differences between types of systems, such as federal versus unitary system, parliamentary versus presidential system or the differences between democratic and totalitarian systems.

Also, the traditional approach is narrow and parochial. Consequently, a large number of works in foreign political systems focused on the analysis of the institutions of government in Western European. This focus was therefore on countries like France, Germany, Belgium, Switzerland, and to a lesser extent the dominion countries and the British Dominions. Various factors comprising the accessibility of the countries studied by the scholars, the relative absence of language difficulties, easy access to necessary and official documents to consult on the countries being studied and other source of materials, as well as cultural affinities, made the focus on European states attractive. Worthy of note, however, is that no systematic effort is made to identify the similarities and differences among these countries except in purely descriptive terms.

The traditional approach is equally static in nature. It is significant to point out that the traditional approach often discountenances the dynamic factors that account for growth and change. The attention of the traditional approach has largely been restricted to what is called political anatomy. After the evolution premises of some of the original works in the nineteenth century were abandoned, students of political institutions apparently lost all interest in the formulation of other theories in the light of which change could be comparatively studies.

The traditional approach has most often appeared as monograph. It is important to note that in the study of foreign governments, while a large volume has been written, the greatest percentage has been in form of monographs. The monograph has largely focused on the study of the political institutions of system or on the discussion of a particular institution in a system.

b) The Institutional Approach

When it dawned on the political scientists that legal codes or frameworks and the constitution are too narrow to capture politics in its entirety, a shift in emphasis became inevitable. The necessity to study political relations was believed to be the central theme of politics, rather than just its history or legal manifestations. By this, therefore, the basic and most evident realities of political studies focused essentially on political institutions, namely, legislatures, executives and courts. At this stage, some rudimentary kind of empirical study became manifest. This is what has been described as naïve empiricism. Despite the seeming application of rudimentary empiricism, the work done by institutionalists is mainly descriptive. Indeed, the comprehensive description of political institutions, rather than offering an analytical explanation of the political systems, is the goal of the institutionalists. For instance, the legal power, responsibilities and functions of the assembly might be listed and described.

Mary Douglas and Aron Wildavsky (1983) vision the role of institutions as problem-simplifying devices arguing that individuals delegate their decision-making processes to the institutions (Douglas and Wildavsky, 1983). Hence, for Douglas and Wildavsky institutions would succeed when they are based on natural structures. However, Pierre Bourdieu argues that institutions would succeed when they are based on practice (Bourdieu, 1990).

CHAPTER SEVEN

7.1. The Logic of Comparative Political Inquiry

Meaning of Paradigms, Abstraction and Logic

According to Michael Sodaro (2001), the term paradigm has two connotations in political science. In one sense, a paradigm is a prime example of a particular phenomenon or pattern. Paradigms are quite useful in comparative politics because they help us observe and analyze variations on a theme. In this circumstance, paradigms serve the same purpose with models in summary; a paradigm is a particular way of looking at phenomena, formulating questions and generalizations, and conducting scientific research. The second dimension of a paradigm focuses on a particular forum of intellectual inquiry or a specific approach to scientific investigation. Moreover, a paradigm in the context of political science is akin to essential features to rules of scientific logic that evolved from empirical approaches to scientific enquiry, championed by Copernicus, Newton and other contributors to modern science. In the earlier years, the dominant paradigm of political research tilted towards descriptive modes of analysis with inclinations and emphasis on governmental institutions and constitutional law. It was not so much concerned with the study of how people behave in political life. Scientific thinking in this time did not employ concepts such as variables, hypotheses and correlations.

7.2. Abstraction and Logic in Comparative Political Analysis

The word abstraction is from abstract which has to do with general principles or theories rather than specific instances. Thus, abstraction as a generalizing idea or theory developed from concrete examples of events. The term *"logic"* originated from Greek word *"logike"* meaning the art and science of reasoning. It is the formal systematic study of the principles of valid inference and correct reasoning. Logic as a discipline dates back to Aristotle, who established its fundamental place in philosophy. Logic concerns the structure of statements and arguments, in formal systems of inference and natural language. Logic is often associated today with argumentation theory. It is often said that its logical form determines the validity of an argument, not by its content.

The behavioral method to political studies has led to the introduction of logic in politics. Logic is an integral part of mathematics and computer science. The advent of behavioral method has led to the introduction of quantitative method of analysis in political studies. However, the introduction of this method has resulted into contention about which mode of analysis is superior between the advocates of quantitative and qualitative approaches to political science. Quantitatively inclined analysts cherish the precision and neatness of statistical rigor; they deride qualitatively oriented researcher as vague. Conversely, qualitatively oriented political scientists accuse their number-crunching quantitative colleagues (quant political scientists) of ignoring everything about politics that cannot be reduced to mere statistics. Thus, they accused quantifiers of failing to appreciate the full scope of political reality in all its complexity. However, a good number of political scientists today agree that quantitative and qualitative approaches are complementary and that the approach an analyst uses depends on the nature of the problem being studied. It is essential to note that, which both quantitative and qualitative approaches use scientific analysis, both must observe the ground rules of scientific logic.

7.3. Paths in Political Logic

Basically, there are two broad paths on the road of political inquiry, namely, the normative and the empirical approach. The normative approach focuses on philosophy, values and norms. The empirical approach relies on measurements and observation rather than theory or norm.

Empirical Approaches

According to Arend Lighphart (2010), there are four basic methods of discovering and establishing general empirical prepositions (Lighphart, 2010). One of these methods is experimental, while the other three are non-experimental. The non-experimental methods are the case study, the statistical method and the comparative method. The case study method involves the intensive study of individual cases. Statistical methods involve more sophisticated forms of measurement and observation: public opinion polls, survey research, and various other forms of quantitative measures are used to help make the measurement and observation that is characteristics of the empirical approach even more accurate. The comparative method may be likened to two or more case studies put together. We focus upon a particular political structure or behavior and examine it from comparative perspective. We look for similarities, and differences in different settings, or we may do our comparison in one setting but compare across timelines and series. This is called diachronic comparison. For example, we may compare Nigeria's legislature in 2023 with that of 2013 and 2003 in order to observe differences in the relative power and structures of that legislature. Or we may compare institutions or behavior at one point in time thus synchronic comparisons that compare across national borders, for example, examining the role of the legislature in Nigeria with the role of the legislature in the United States of America and Australia.

Logical Fallacies in Comparative Political Analysis

It is necessary to stress that the application of logic has to do with critical thinking about life and in this book, it is something to do with politics. However, there are certain logical fallacies that are commonly committed in political argumentation which we must avoid in making comparisons in politics (Sodaro, 2001). These include:

i. Fallacy of Composition

This error is often committed when we assume that the whole is exactly the same as its parts. For instance, ascribing attributes such as attitudes, behaviors, etc to an entire class or group when those attributes may only apply to a portion of the group. A relevant example is "South Sudanese are very violent" when in fact only some South Sudanese maybe violent while others are not at all.

ii. Tautology (Circular Reasoning)

Tautology comes from the Greek word for "the same". It has to do with ascribing causation to the very phenomenon that we are trying to explain it causes such as dependent variable as an independent variable that accounts for it. Here's an example "countrywide armed conflict between the government and opposition groups in Yugoslavia' produced a bitter civil war". The statement is tautological because civil war is itself a countrywide armed conflict between the government and opposition groups. The two points are essentially the same thing, as one cannot cause the other. Michael Sodaro (2001) continued by saying that one of the most famous tautologies ever attributed to a politician was the remark attributed to President Calvin Coolidge of United States, "when people are unable to find work, unemployment results" (Sodaro, 2001).

iii. Post Hoc Ergo Propter Hoc

"After it, therefore because of it" is the fallacy of concluding that A caused B just because A preceded B. for example, "The U.S led victory over Iraq in the Persian Gulf war at the start of 1991, precipitated the collapse of the Soviet Union later that same year". The statement as argued by Sodaro (2001) does not explain why the war was a cause of the USSR's demise but simply assume that it was. In fact, the war cannot be said to have had demonstrable effect on the collapse of the Soviet Union.

iv. A Fortiori (All the More)

A fortiori assumes that what is true of a phenomenon at one level or degree automatically is true of the same phenomenon at larger levels or degrees. For instance, "the more private enterprise there is in the economy, the more democracy will flourish.", Assumes without empirical validation, that, because a certain amount of private enterprise maybe good for democracy, then a complete private economy, without the involvement of government in economic affairs whatsoever will be better for democracy. If that is done there will be a wide credibility gap between the poor and the rich.

v. False Analogy

A false analogy is an error of making inappropriate or inexact analogies or comparison between one phenomenon or situation and another. For instance, political systems, are like an organism; they are born, they grow, and they inevitably decay and die. This organic analogy does not stand up to the reality. Analogies that refer to similar historical events are often misused as well. For example, the Persian Gulf War was exactly like World War II, Saddam Hussein was another Hitler, and Hitler showed that dictators must not be appeased. Although some similarities can be obvious, they cannot be assumed. They are exactly the same.

vi. Non-Falsiable

It is only hypotheses that can be tested empirically that are capable of being contradicted by factual evidence. An example of a non-falsifiable hypothesis is "the laws of history make the collapse of capitalism inevitable in the long run, though it may succeed in the short run." Since it is impossible to have empirical evidence of the future, we have no basis for proving the rightness or wrongness of the hypothesis. It cannot be empirically tested.

vii. False Inference

This is the fallacy of making unwarranted inferences from statistical data or other facts, especially when trying to establish causation.

viii. Reductivism.

This is the error of explaining something in terms of one sole cause when other causes could also be at work.

CHAPTER EIGHT

Comparative Democratization

8.1. Definition of Democracy

Democracy is a government of the people, by the people and for the people (Lincoln, 1865). It is etymologically from the Greek *"demos"* referring to the 'people' and *"kratia"* meaning the 'rule'. Thus, Greek argues it as the 'rule of the commoners. Thus, modern political democracy is a system of governance in which rulers are held accountable for their actions in the public realm by citizens, acting indirectly through the competition and cooperation of their elected representatives (Schimitter & Karl, 1991).

Democracy is by far the most challenging form of government - both for politicians and for the people. The so-called "democracies" in classical antiquity (Athens and Rome) represent precursors of modern democracies. Like modern democracy, they were created as a reaction to a concentration and abuse of power by the rulers. Yet the theory of modern democracy was not formulated until the Age of Enlightenment (17th and 18th centuries), when philosophers defined the essential elements of democracy: separation of powers, basic civil rights and human rights, religious liberty and separation of church and state

Although democracy is highly praised as the best form of the government, Winston Churchill argues as it as "the worst form of the government, except for all others that have been tried" (Churchill,

1948). Robert Dahl refers it as "majoritarian tyranny" (Dahl, 2009). Nicholas Eberstadt views it as "tyranny of numbers or misrule by the numbers" (Eberstadt, 1995).

On the other hand, democratization is the process where democracy takes place. It moves from building democracy to democratic transition and then consolidation.

One of the major themes throughout the democracy literature is that it does not consist of a single unique set of institutions. There are many types of democracy, and their diverse practices produce a similarly varied set of effects. The specific form of democracy is contingent upon a country's socioeconomic conditions as well as it's entrenched on state structures and policy practices.

A regime or system of governance is an ensemble of patterns that determines the methods of access to the principal public offices; the characteristics of the actors admitted to or excluded from such access; the strategies that actors may use to gain access; and the rules that are followed in the making of publicly binding decisions. To work properly, the ensemble must be institutionalized. That is to say, the various patterns must be habitually known, practiced, and accepted by most, if not all, actors. Increasingly, the preferred mechanism of institutionalization is a written body of laws undergirded by a written constitution, though many enduring political norms can have an informal, prudential, or traditional basis.

For the sake of economy and comparison, these forms, characteristics, and rules are usually bundled together and given a generic label. Democracy is one; others are autocratic, authoritarian, despotic, dictatorial, tyrannical, totalitarian, absolutist, traditional, monarchic, oligarchic, plutocratic, aristocratic, and sultanistic. Each of these regime forms may in turn be broken down into sub-types.

Like all regimes, democracies depend upon the presence of rulers, persons who occupy specialized authority roles and can give legitimate commands to others. What distinguishes democratic rulers from non-democratic ones are the norms that condition how the former come to power and the practices that hold them accountable for their actions.

The public realm encompasses the making of collective norms and choices that are binding on the society and backed by state coercion. Its content can vary a great deal across democracies, depending upon pre-existing distinctions between the public and the private, state and society, legitimate coercion and voluntary exchange, and collective needs and individual preferences. The liberal conception of democracy advocates circumscribing the public realm as narrowly as possible, while the socialist or social-democratic approach would extend that realm through regulation, subsidization, and, in some cases, collective ownership of property. Neither is intrinsically more democratic than the other-just differently democratic. This implies that measures aimed at "developing the private sector" are no more democratic than those aimed at-"developing the public sector." Both, if carried to extremes, could undermine the practice of democracy, the former by destroying the basis for satisfying collective needs and exercising legitimate authority; the latter by destroying the basis for satisfying individual preferences and controlling illegitimate government actions. Differences of opinion over the optimal mix of the two provide much of the substantive content of political conflict within established democracies.

Indeed, citizens are the most distinctive element in democracies. All regimes have rulers and a public realm, but only to the extent that they are democratic if do they have citizens. Historically, severe restrictions on citizenship were imposed in most emerging or partial democracies according to criteria of age, gender, class, race, literacy, property ownership, tax-paying status, and so on. Only a small part of the total population was eligible to vote or run for office. Only restricted social categories were allowed to form, join, or support political associations. After protracted struggles, in some cases involving violent domestic upheaval or international war, - most of these restrictions were lifted. Today, the criteria for inclusion are fairly standard. All native-born adults are eligible, although somewhat higher age limits may still be imposed upon candidates for certain offices. Unlike the early American and European democracies of the nineteenth century, none of the recent democracies in southern Europe, Latin America, Asia, or Eastern Europe has even attempted to impose formal restrictions on the franchise or eligibility to office.

Competition has not always been considered an essential defining condition of democracy. "Classic" democracies presumed decision making based on direct participation leading to consensus. The assembled citizenry was expected to agree on a common course of action after listening to the alternatives and weighing their respective merits and demerits.

Majority rule is also associated with democracy as discussed above. Any governing body that makes decisions by combining the votes of more than half of those eligible and present is said to be democratic, whether that majority emerges within an electorate, a parliament, a committee, a city council, or a party caucus. For exceptional purposes (for example, amending the constitution or expelling a member), "qualified majorities" of more than 50 percent may be required, but few would deny that democracy must involve some means of aggregating the equal preferences of individuals.

A problem arises, however, when numbers meet intensities. What happens when a properly assembled majority (especially a stable, self-perpetuating one) regularly makes decisions that harm some minority (especially a threatened cultural or ethnic group)? In these circumstances, successful democracies tend to qualify the central principle of majority rule in order to protect minority rights. Such qualifications can take the form of constitutional provisions that place certain matters beyond the reach of majorities (bills of rights); requirements for concurrent majorities in several different constituencies (confederalism); guarantees securing the autonomy of local or regional governments against the demands of the central authority (federalism); grand coalition governments that incorporate all parties (consociation-alism); or the negotiation of social pacts between major social groups like business and labour (neo-corporatism). The most common and effective way of protecting minorities, however, lies in the everyday operation of interest associations and social movements.

Cooperation has always been a central feature of democracy. Actors must voluntarily make collective decisions binding on the polity as a whole. They must cooperate in order to compete. They must be capable of acting collectively through parties, associations, and movements in order to select candidates, articulate preferences, petition authorities, and influence policies.

In contemporary political discourse, this phenomenon of cooperation and deliberation via autonomous group activity goes under the rubric of "civil society." The civil society advocates for diverse units of social identity and interest of the society, independent of the state (and perhaps even of parties).

Representatives of the people whether directly or indirectly do elect their leaders and they do most of the real work in modeen democracies. Most of these representatives are professional politicians who orient their careers around the desire to fill key offices. It is doubtful that any democracy could survive without such people. The central question, therefore, is not whether or not there will be a political elite or even a professional political class, but how these representatives are chosen and then held accountable for their actions.

On the doctrine separation of powers, democracy strives when the three branches of the government namely, executive, legislature and judiciary are independent from one another and not interfere with by any force.

8.2 Procedures that Make Democracy Possible

The defining components of democracy are necessarily abstract and may give rise to a considerable variety of institutions and sub-types of democracy. For democracy to thrive, however, specific procedural norms must be followed and civic rights must be respected. Any polity that fails to impose such restrictions upon itself and that fails to follow the "rule of law" with regard to its own procedures, should not be considered democratic. These procedures alone do not define democracy, but their presence is indispensable to its persistence. In essence, they are necessary but not sufficient conditions for its existence.

Robert Dahl (1989) has offered the most generally accepted listing of what he terms the "procedural minimal" conditions that must be present for modem political democracy (or as he puts it, "polyarchy") to exist:

1. Control over government decisions about policy is constitutionally vested in elected officials;
2. Elected officials are chosen in frequent and fairly conducted elections in which coercion is comparatively uncommon;
3. Practically all adults have the right to vote in the election of officials;
4. Practically all adults have the fight to run for elective offices in the government;
5. Citizens have a fight to express themselves without the danger of severe punishment on broadly defined political matters;
6. Citizens have a fight to seek out alternative sources of information. Moreover, alternative sources of information exist and are protected by law; and
7. Citizens also have the fight to form relatively independent associations or organizations, including independent political parties and interest groups or CSOs (Dahl, 1989).

These seven conditions seem to capture the essence of procedural democracy for many theorists, but I propose to add two others. The first might be thought of as a further refinement of item (1), while the second might be called an implicit prior condition to all seven of the above.

Popularly elected officials must be able to exercise their constitutional powers without being subjected to overriding (albeit informal) opposition from unelected officials. Democracy is in jeopardy if military officers, entrenched civil servants, or state managers retain the capacity to act independently of elected civilians or even veto decisions made by the people's representatives. Without this additional caveat, the militarized polities of contemporary South America, where civilian control over the military does not exist and might be classified by many scholars as democracies, just as they have been (with the exception of Nicaragua) by US policymakers. The caveat thus guards against what we earlier called "electoralism" the tendency to focus on the holding of elections while ignoring other political realities (Schimitter & Karl, 1991).

8. The polity must be self-governing: It must be able to act independently of constraints imposed by some other overarching political system. Dahl (1989) and other contemporary democratic theorists probably took this condition for granted since they referred to formally sovereign nation-states.

9. Elite theorists believe that only a limited form of democracy is possible in the above context. We participate only once every four or five years or so, yet elections for choosing leaders are key method (Kissane, 2012). These elections give legitimacy to policy, which is made by bureaucrats. Competition (between elites) is the key value not participation. In this system, the ability to remove unpopular leaders without bloodshed is the key virtue.

Dahl's Oligarchy as Response to Elite Theory

No governing elite (polyarchy; not rule of the few but many). Polyarchy a system of popular control of elites.

8.3. Democracy and Types of Political Systems

As I have defined democracy as above, it is also important to define political systems, according to renowned political scientists, Gabriel Almond and James Coleman (1960), "political systems are systems of interactions to be found in all independent polities which perform the functions of integration and adaptation by means of legitimate physical compulsion" (Almond and Coleman, 1960).

The Concise Oxford Dictionary of Political Science (1994) defines political systems as "any persistent pattern of human relationship that involves (to a significant extent) power, rule and authority" (Oxford Dictionary, 1182). It is a collectivity of political institutions (for example, government), associations (for instance, political parties) and organizations performing roles based on a set of norms and goals (like maintaining internal order, regulating foreign relations, etc.). Sociologically, the term 'political system' refers to the social institution which relies on a recognized set of procedures for implementing and achieving the political goals of a community or society. In nutshell, political systems are vehicles and tools of running states and governments.

Table 1: Types of Political Systems

System	Description	Example (s)
Monarchy	A political system in which the government is under the control of one powerful leader.	Spain, France & England in 16th -19th Centuries
Constitutional Monarchy	A government in which leadership rests in the hands of representative system based on a written constitution, with a monarch (king or queen) as a respected figurehead.	Great Britain, Western Europe and much of South East Asia, Central Asia and Middle East Countries.

Limited Monarchy	A government headed by a King or queen who possesses limited power which is usually shared with some type of legislative body, such as a parliament.	England after the Glorious Revolution
Oligarchy	A political system in which the government is under the control of few individuals (often very rich).	Ancient Sparta
Theocracy	A political system in which the government is under the control of a religious organization or its officials.	Modern day Iran
Aristocracy	A political system in which the government is under the control of wealthy landowners.	France before the French Revolution
Democracy	A political system in which the government is under the control of the citizens themselves, or elected representatives chosen from eligible citizens.	Ancient Greece, Modern day India, Australia, Europe and North America
Parliamentary Democracy	The English system of government since the Glorious Revolution of 1688, when the divine right of kings came to an end and Parliament was considered the supreme law-making body. Members of Parliament represented the people and made the laws	Great Britain, India, Australia, Japan

Representative Democracy	A form of government in which power and responsibility are held by elected officials, placed there by the vote of the citizens, i.e., essentially all individuals over a particular age, without restrictions regarding gender, colour, religion, or properly ownership. The representatives represent the citizens.	Great Britain
Direct Democracy	A form of government in which power and responsibility are held by citizens who vote in their leaders. They can easily remove these leaders through riots/demonstrations or parliaments' impeachments. Citizens influence the functioning of the government.	United States of America
Absolutism	A political system in which kings and queens have a complete control over government and the lives of their subjects.	France under Louis XIV, Russia under Czars
Feudalism	A social, political and economic system that dominated all aspects of medieval life. Strong local lords formed a strict code of behaviour and allegiances that became the foundation of feudal life.	Europe and Japan during the Middle Ages

Dictatorship	Form of government in which all power is held by one person or a small group.	North Korea, Sudan, South Sudan, Uganda Zimbabwe, Eritrea
Totalitarianism	An ideology where all social, economic, and political powers are centred in the government completely.	USSR under Joseph Stalin
Communism	A system of government in which a single, totalitarian, party holds power. It is characterized by state control of the economy and restriction on personal freedoms. It was first proposed by Karl Marx and Friedrich Engels in *The Communist Manifesto*	China, Former Soviet Union, Vietnam, Cuba, North Korea
Socialism	A political system where the means of production are controlled by the workers and all things are shared evenly. Socialist policies provide for government for government funding of many basic needs such as food, shelter and medical care	Tanzania under Mwalimu Julius Nyerere, Sweden, Denmark, Norway, Finland
Fascism	A system of government that promotes extreme nationalism, repression, anti-communism, and is ruled by a dictator	East Germany under Hitler, USSR under Mussolini, Spain under Franco

Constructed by the author

8.4. Transitology I: Structuralist Approaches

Since the "concept of transitology" is prevalent within the literature of democratization, it's essential to get a working definition of transition to democracy so that a clear cut is drawn from mere concept of democratization. There is much scholarly debate over the most useful definition of "democratic transition". However, O'Donnell and Schmitter, Linz & Stephan and Carothers (1986) make constructive arguments. O'Donnell & Schmitter define transition as the interval between one political system and another (O'Donnell & Schmitter, 1986). According to them, the beginning and end of this process are relatively easy to trace. The transition begins with a split in the authoritarian regime, after which regime elites who believe in the necessity of electoral legitimating become dominant. These soft-liners, as they are known, typically negotiate a pact with moderate opposition elites, providing for elections under clearly defined rules and procedures. The transition ends when new political elites assume power or, in rare cases, the old elites are newly legitimized.

In most sub-Saharan African cases, as well as many elsewhere, both boundaries of the transition process are in fact hard to delimit. It is difficult to determine when a particular transition began and, more significantly, when it has actually ended (Brown, 2004).

Thomas Carother's view on the transition paradigm refers transition to democracy where the process of democratization is assumed to include some redesign of state institutions such as the creation of new electoral institutions, parliamentary reforms, and judicial reforms as well as a modification of already functioning states (Carothers, 2002). Linz and Stephan provide an in-depth definition by noting that a democratic transition is complete when the sufficient agreement has been reached about political procedures to produce an elected government, when a government comes to power that is the direct result of a free and popular vote, meaning this government has the de facto has the authority to generate new policies, and when the executive, legislative and judicial bodies generated by the new democracy do not have to share power with other bodies de jure (Linz & Stephan, 1996).

Structuralist Approaches

The structural approaches are measured by three power structures: state, class, and transnational power. Rueschemeyer, Stephen, and Stephen in *Capitalist Development and Democracy* introduce a "three power structures" model in which the interaction between state, class, and transnational power structures shape the societal and political outcomes (Rueschemeyer et al., 1992). In this view, the state structure is of great significance in promoting or preventing change toward democracy transition; there is a correlation between the paths toward democratization of the state and the type of regime. There is also a correlation between democratization and the socioeconomic structure. The success or the failure of democratization depends largely on the extent to which social groups and classes have equal and sufficient access to the state resources. Finally, the structure of international politics contributes to the politics of democratization and de-democratization.

Rueschemeyer et al (1992), in spite of limitations, has successfully synthesized three structural theories of social change: modernization theories, dependency / world system theories, and Barrington Moore's structural-historical approach. These three theories provide us with a wide-ranging structural argument that takes into account the interaction of internal and external structures and social (class) and political (state) factors. The authors reject either optimism of modernization theories (linear-universalism) or pessimism of dependency / world system theories (negative correlations between dependency on the one hand and development and democracy on the other). They follow Barrington Moore's particularistic tradition in which a positive correlation exists between capitalist development and democracy only under particular class structure. Rueschemer et al (1992) advance Moore's historical-structural tradition by including two more structural factors: state and transnational power. Yet, like most structural accounts, capitalist development and democracy pays less attention to the role of political agency in social change and regime transformation.

From this integrative perspective, structures both enable and limit human agency. they operate as environments that delimit the range of possible actions without determining action. From this perspective, people act through structures, rather than structures acting through people. In other words, actors can choose how to use structural resources and potentially improve these resources.

8.5. Transitology II: Agency Approaches

The agency is examined in terms of leadership capability (individual level), the organizational arrangements (institutional level), and the intellectual discourse (cultural/ideological level). Human choices and the very concept of leadership suggest that individual/political agents can make a significant difference in democratic transition. Political agency, however, is very much affected by balance of power, both among social and political forces. Democratic transition, as Tatu in Vanhanen (2002) observes, "will take place under conditions in which power resources are so widely distributed that no (social or political) group is any longer able to suppress its competitors or to maintain its hegemony" (Vanhanen, 2002).

On this synthetic and dialectical view, individuals, ideas, and, to use Barrington Moore's words, "cultural values do not descend from heaven to influence the course of history" (Moore, 1966). They are rooted in and influenced by social structures. Yet, if you ever doubted the importance of the individual in history, writes Timothy Garton Ash, "consider the story of Ayatollah Khomeini": An old man who invented a new and modern political system founded on an old and apolitical concept of *velayat-e faqih* (guardianship of jurist). This political system, which would not exist without him, is *"Khomeinism"* (Ash, 2005).

In nutshell, both structuralist and agency approaches have endeavoured to promote democratic transitions. Nonetheless, other theoretical overarching such as modernization and elite approaches continues to dominate the literature of transitology.

8.6. Consolidation/Consolidology, Gray Zone and Hybrid Regimes

With the extension of democracy to additional countries now becoming slowed, political scientists and political actors in new democracies have been increasingly focused on what has come to be called 'democratic consolidation' or 'consolidology' (Schedler, 1998). Originally, the term 'consolidology' was meant to describe the challenge of making new democracies secure, of extending their life expectancy beyond the short, of making them immune against the threat of authoritarian regression, of building dams against the eventual "reverse waves". To this original mission, democracy is become "the only game in town". Countless other tasks have been added to mean that democracy is the "only bull in town" and it has compounded conundrums. As a result, the list of "problems of democratic consolidation" (as well as the corresponding list of 'conditions of democratic' consolidation') has expanded beyond all recognition. It has come to include the following divergent items according to Andreas Schedler (1998):

- Popular legitimation
- The diffusion of democratic values
- The neutralization of anti-systems actors
- Civilian supremacy over military
- The elimination of authoritarian enclaves
- Party building and consensus

- The organization of functional interests
- The stabilization of electoral rules
- The routinization of politics
- The decentralization of state power
- The introduction of mechanisms of direct democracy
- Judicial reforms
- The alleviation of poverty
- Economic stabilization

The application of consolidology depends on where we stand, what Schedler (1998) called "our empirical viewpoints" and where we are going, that he also called "our normative horizon".

From Schedler thinking, democratic consolidation or consolidology emerged as a concept interpreted and edited by individual democratic scholars.

Larry Diamond (2003) adds that consolidation is the deepening of democracy to include both elites and masses agreement on government functions (Diamond, 2003). Diamond further argues that consolidology is achieved if a state conducts three free and fair elections consecutively. However, Diamond has forgotten to acknowledge that elections alone doesn't carry enough weight for measuring consolidation.

On the other hand, Guillermo O'Donnell (1996) argues that when the elections are institutionized then they are taken as stabilized process of promoting democracy and at such a country can be called as democratically consolidated (O'Donnell, 1996). O'Donnell brightly introduced a phrase called *"democratic persistence"* referring to "end product of a long democratization processes". Adam Przeworski argues that democratic consolidation occurs "when no one can imagine acting outside the democratic institutions" (Przeworkski, 2003).

Besides, Juan J. Linz and Afred Stephan (1996) argue that nothing can promote democratic consolidation unless there is an existence of the following:

a. State thus as the maxim *"No state no democracy"*
b. Free, fair and contested elections (that meets Robert Dahl's attributes)
c. The need for the regime's leaders to be democratic.

Hence the conditions for democratic consolidation according Linz and Stephan should include amongst others:
a. Valued political society
b. Rule of law
c. State bureaucracy
d. Institutionalized economic society
e. Active and lively civil society

Thus, we can have positive consolidation/consolidology. For example, maximalist approach and negative consolidation/consolidology and the minimalist approach. Consolidation is when democracy is the only game in town as argued earlier.

Problems with the concept of consolidation/consolidology:
i. It is based on consensus
ii. It is ethnocentric since it is European's centred
iii. It lacks cutting points such as measurement, control and predictions. Indeed, there is no clear-cut threshold
iv. The literature is teleology. For example, fixed assumption on consolidation as a natural process. For instance, Britain is consolidated but people are not consolidated given their different views on democracy.

The Gray Zone
Gray zones or areas are referred as incomplete democracies (O'Donnell, 1996). The bulk of the contemporary scholarly literature tells us that these 'incomplete democracies' are failing to become consolidated,

or institutionalized. By far the majority of third-wave countries have not achieved relatively well-functioning democracy or do not seem to be deepening or advancing whatever democratic progress they have made. In a small number of countries, initial political openings have clearly failed and authoritarian regimes have re-solidified, as in Uzbekistan, Turkmensistan, Belarus, Togo, Kenya, Uganda and Egypt. Most of the "transitional countries", however, are neither dictatorial nor clearly headed toward democracy (Carothers, 2002). They have entered a political *gray zone,* of what Larry Diamond called a "twilight zone" (Diamond, 2003). They have some tributes of democratic political life, including at least limited political space for opposition parties and independent civil society, as well as regular elections and democratic constitutions. Yet, they suffer from serious democratic deficits, often including poor representation of citizens' interests, low levels of political participation beyond voting, frequent abuse of the law by the government officials, elections of uncertain legitimacy, very low levels of public confidence in state institutions, and persistently poor institutional performance by the state (Carothers, 2002).

Hybrid Regimes

These are regimes that are less than electoral democracies, they are competitive authoritarian systems and hegemonic-party systems (Diamond, 2003). At best, Ukraine, Nigeria, and Venezuela are ambiguous cases. Although these are hardly the only issues or anomalies in regime classification. In the 1990 and 2000s, scholars and observers debated whether Mexico, Senegal, and Singapore were really democracies (as their governments insisted). These debates fizzled once other countries in their respective regions began to experience true democratization and the democratic deficiencies of these one-party hegemonies became more blatantly apparent. More recently, a growing number of scholars are questioning the tendency to classify regimes as democratic simply because they have multiparty elections with some degree of competition and uncertainty. In an important contribution focused on Eurasia and Latin America, Steven Levitsky and Lucan Way (2018) argue that regimes may be both competitive and authoritarian and these regimes end up as hybrid regimes (Levitsky and Way, 2018).

Hybrid regimes (combining democratic and authoritarian elements) are not new. For instance, in 1960s and 1970s, there existed multi-party, electoral, but then these regimes turned out to be undemocratic regimes. Of these electoral autocracies—Mexico, Singapore, Malaysia, Senegal, South Africa, Rhodesia, and Taiwan (which allowed *dangwai,* or "outside the party," competitors) - only the Malaysian and Singaporean regimes survive today. Historically, there have also been numerous cases in Europe and Latin America of limited (elite) party competition with a limited franchise. In Latin America, these nineteenth-century and early-twentieth-century "oligarchical" democracies "contributed to the ultimate development of full democracy" by establishing some of its major political institutions, as well as the principles of limitation and rotation of power (Linz and Stepan, 1996). Thus, these countries epitomized Dahl's optimal path to stable polyarchy, with the rise of political competition preceding the expansion of participation, so that the culture of democracy first took root among a small elite and then diffused to the larger population as it was gradually incorporated into electoral politics (Dahl, 2009). In the contemporary world of mass participation, this gradualist path has been closed off, and anxious elites have thus sought out other ways to limit and control competition.

8.7. Authoritarian Resilience

Authoritarianism is defined as form of government that is autocratic, dictatorial and oppressive. It is a government that doesn't provide rights and freedoms to the citizens (the populace) (Diamond, 2003). Resilience on the other hand is defined as a withering off the political change by the system that has debuted itself (Gallagher and Hanson, 2013).

Hence, authoritarian resilience is when the autocratic, repressive and terror of activities of the regime entrenched themselves and cannot be changed by any political transformation. It is when regimes defy Western democratization in the first wave, second wave, third wave and fourth wave of democratization (Huntington, 1993).

Several decades ago, political scientists described the Soviet Union and other European Communist regimes using similar terms. However, the stability of these regimes was performance-based. As long as they could fulfil their social contract, the regimes remained resilient. When lack of growth made the provision of social spending unsustainable, these regimes were weakened and eventually collapsed. Yet, Cuba and North Korea survived severe economic challenges in the 1990s. A theory of communist resilience should be able to explain these divergent outcomes.

The successful and adaptive resilience of China and Vietnam appears to have more in common with the developmental path of capitalist autocracies in the same region than with the other surviving communist states of North Korea and Cuba. The resilience of the Vietnamese and Chinese Communist Parties may be explained by reasons that do not extend to the survival of the North Korean and Cuban regimes. In other words, we make a distinction between regime resilience and survival. Survival is simply a matter of maintaining power over an extended period of time (Gallagher and Hanson, 2013). Resilient regimes, however, not only survive but also thrive and adapt while fostering the growth of national military and economic power. They remain the unchallenged authority during periods of significant social and economic change. Thus, Logic of Political Survival (*LPS*) has been the order of the day for the Chinese, Vietnamese, Cubans, North Koreans, Venezuelans and even the Great Soviet Governments.

As Clarke and Stone (2011) argued when presented a detailed analysis of the statistical findings in the Logic of Political Survival (LPS), the duo concluded:

The Logic of Political Survival makes the arresting claim that it has isolated the key mechanism by which democracy generates its benefits, thereby resolving the debate between the advocates of institutions, behaviour, and political culture (Clarke and Stone, 2011).

But studies have shown that numerous dictators have pursued economic development policies so that they stay afloat amongst the citizenry. As Adam Przeworski et al (2000) argues:

> Much of the appeal of dictatorships stems from the fact that at various moments they have seemed to offer "the best practice." The "tigers" have tended to be dictatorships. But are dictatorships necessarily tigers? The list of disasters generated by authoritarianism is long and tragic. . . For every developmental miracle, there have been several dictatorships that have engaged in grandiose projects that have ended in ruin, or else dictatorships that have simply stolen and squandered opportunities (Prezeworski, 2000).

The Chinese case, in particular, represents a dictatorship that has produced both catastrophic developmental tragedy (the great leap forward famine) and impressive developmental achievements under the rule of the same party. In the 1990s, China scholars followed the collapse of the Soviet Union with musings and debates on whether the Chinese empire would suffer the same fate. We now see more and more arguments that probe the Chinese body politic for its mystery of "authoritarian resilience" (Nathan, 2003). This is because most authoritarian regimes try to balance goods provision with repression but only some, perhaps even only a few, have the institutional capacity to do so efficiently (Gallagher & Hanson, 2013).

As Barbara Geddes (1999) notes in her study of variation across authoritarian regimes, "single-party regimes survive in part because their institutional structures make it relatively easy for them to allow greater participation and popular influence on policy without giving up their dominant role in the political system" (Geddes, 1999). Although she points mainly to electoral devices like legalized opposition parties, single-party regimes can also develop other effective institutions, including mass organizations like trade unions, corporatist business associations, government-owned NGOs and parastatals organizations in neighbourhoods, workplaces, and schools. China has used all of these and now also allows competitive elections of village leaders in the countryside. Elected village officials rule in tandem with an appointed Communist Party Secretary.

So, authoritarian resilience is a hard nut to crack for democratizations. Countries that have adopted and survived through authoritarian resilience as discussed above, are not easy to be transformed by any democratic political forces. The authoritarian resilience of North Korea is the reason the United States is at loggerhead with Pyongyang. North Korea too does not appreciate Washington DC's democratic resilience and global dominance and thus rhetoric's between Donald J. Trump and Kim Jong-Un; the supreme leader of North Korea was the order of the 2019. This is the same rhetoric between Putin of Russia and Biden of USA of 2023.

8.8. Conceptual Problems of Regime Type Analyses

The study of democratization presents comparative political scientists with a unique opportunity for theory-building, inviting scholars to understand and explain processes of political regime change and functioning through increasingly broad comparisons, not only encompassing Southern Europe and Latin America, as has been the case in some of the best comparative studies (Linz & Stepan 1996; O'Donnell & Schmitter (1986), but also incorporating cases from Eastern Europe, the former Soviet Union, East Asia, and certain areas of Africa. To seize such an opportunity, however, a comparative political scientist needs both a set of clear and shared concepts that would serve as the foundation for such a research agenda and a simple set of rules concerning how to engage in conceptual "traveling", the use of concepts to study new cases, without falling in the trap of conceptual "stretching", the use of a concept that does not fit the new cases (Collier et al,, 1993).

Conceptual problem of regime - type analysis has been a great conundrum as it is so difficult to comprehend when a regime is absolutely democratic, semi-authoritarian, non-authoritarian or authoritarian. These conceptual issues have not been fully resolved by comparative political scientists, but there is a group of scholars who have made significant contributions to such an agenda in the course of studies that, over a span of thirty years, have sought to account for the breakdown of democracies, the nature of authoritarian regimes, the transitions from authoritarian rule, and the process of democratic consolidation. These scholars include Thomas Carothers, Larry Diamond, David Collier, Robert Dahl, Manuel Antonio Garretón, Arend Lijphart, Juan J. Linz, Guillermo O'Donnell, Adam Przeworski, Philippe Schmitter, Amartya Sen, Alfred Stepan, and Laurence Whitehead amongst others.

Outside of the pioneering work of David Collier (Collier & Mahon 1993; Collier and Levitsky 1997) and the important efforts by Philippe Schmitter to systematize and extend regime analysis as a research programme (Schmitter 1986; Schmitter and Karl 1991), regime analysts have rarely stepped back and taken stock of the concepts that have framed their analysis nor have they addressed their avoidance of the problem of conceptual stretching. The need for such a conceptual analysis is most evident in light of the resistance among specialists on Eastern Europe and the Soviet and post-Soviet cases to embrace the agenda regime analysts developed on the basis of their studies of Southern Europe and Latin America. There are no doubts, a number of reasons for such resistance, but part of the problem appears to be that lack of clarity concerning the key concepts of regime analysis and uncertainty about how to avoid the problem of conceptual stretching has obscured the precise lines along which comparisons are to be carried out. That is, confusion over the concepts that serve to structure and organize comparisons has led many authors to prematurely reject comparisons between the East and the South on the mistaken grounds that the democratization process in Southern European and Latin American is not comparable to the Eastern European and Soviet/Post-Soviet experiences. If a dialogue among specialists focusing on different regions and countries, an essential precondition for the accumulation of knowledge, is to be possible and if the study of democratization is to deliver the theoretical rewards it appears to offer, it is necessary, therefore, to clarify these conceptual issues for the purpose of eschewing comparative conundrums (Munick, 1996).

Political Regime Type as a Two-Dimensional Concept Analysis

The basic reason why regime analysis constitutes a coherent agenda is that it has, for the most part, formulated a variety of concepts that have retained a common overarching concept: the concept of political regime type. That is, whether analysts have focused on the study of democracy or authoritarianism, on problems of transition or consolidation, their work has been conceived with reference to a broader and more encompassing notion of political regime type or some other concepts, such as form of government or system of government, which has been used interchangeably with a political regime type. Nonetheless, very rarely do regime analysts stop to define what they mean by political regime type and even more rarely do they actually consider how the definition of political regime type they implicitly or explicitly adopt can serve as a tool to organize their inquiries. On the basis of a reconstruction of the concept of political regime type, it is possible to identify attributes that recur in the definitions that have been proposed by regime political analysts. Moreover, further consideration indicates that it is possible to go beyond the simple enumeration of attributes and show that these attributes actually form two neat groups. What emerges from the collection and organization of definitions, indeed, is a two-dimensional concept, consisting of a procedural and a behavioural dimension.

The first procedural dimension concerns a set of rules or procedures, an aspect that regime political analysts have addressed when they state precisely what issues these procedural rules determine. This is a relatively uncomplicated aspect of the conceptualization of political regime type. For if there is a slight variation in terms of the specific issues these rules' structure, there is an overall consensus that part of what defines a political regime type are the procedural rules that determine: 1) The number and type of actors who are allowed to gain access to the principal governmental positions, 2) The methods of access to such positions and 3) The rules that are followed in the making of publicly binding decisions (Munick, 1996).

As a point of clarification, it bears stressing that these procedural rules may be formal or informal and explicit or unstated. Procedural rules are contrasted, thus, not to the informal ways in which political power is sometimes actually accessed and exercised, at times despite legal procedures and at other times due to gaps in legal procedures. Rather, procedures are counter-posed to outcomes. This is an important point because the inclusion of informal rules as part of the definition of political regime type provides a conceptualization that is not restricted to formal legal analysis but that seeks to address actual practices, whether they are legally sanctioned or not and whether they correspond to formal political institutions or not.

If this first and procedural dimension is generally seen as the central aspect of a definition of political regime type, to the extent that procedural rules concerning the establishment and conduct of government are sometimes emphasized to the exclusion of any other factors, there is also a behavioural component to the concept of political regime type.

This second dimension draws attention to the importance of actors and to a simple but extremely consequential point: that procedural rules structure and shape the conduct of politics only inasmuch as actors accept or comply with these rules, thus behaviour.

By way of summary, the concept of a political regime type that underpins the agenda of regime analysis is hereby defined, on the one hand, by the procedural rules and actors behavioural engagement, whether formal or informal, that determine the number and type of actors who are allowed to gain access to the principal governmental positions, the methods of access to such positions, and the rules that are followed in the making of publicly binding decisions, and, on the other hand, by the strategic acceptance of these rules by all major political actors and the lack of normative rejection of these rules by any major political actor.

8.9. Political Transformation in World Politics

The argument for political transformation in world politics commenced with the ending of Second World War and ushering in of Cold War period. Now the question here is, what happened after the Cold War? As it is argued in the international relations, Cold War was a global war which was fought through ideologies. There was a need of reconstruction of world order after the Cold War has ended. There were several conferences, meetings, in order to identify the basic dynamics of the new global context. But after 78 years now we can ask to ourselves, was there a restoration of world order within the context of the changes in the post-Cold War situation?

Unfortunately, the answer is no. What happened in last 34 years, now more than 34 years after Cold War? Domestic structures changed in the Balkans and in many other countries. Regional contexts also changed including in the Middle East, Central Asia, Latin America and Africa. The global context has also changed ushering in new challenges.

Our imagination of world politics seventy years ago is vastly different from the era we are currently living today. It was more static, two superpowers, two blocks, dividing almost all regions between those two blocks and with little to compare other lesser nations to those superpowers. Now the situation is much far more dynamic

This political transformation has been captured by the opposing theses of Francis Fukuyama and Samuel Huntington. *"The End of History and the Last Man"* published in 1992 is a captivating work stemming from a 1989 article, *"End of History"* published in 1989 in Journal of International Affairs. Fukuyama and Huntington argued that with the collapse of communist regimes in the 1990s, then history ended. However, Ahmet Davutoğlu, a Turkish scholar retorted that *"History Will Not End"* that *"The history will flow faster than before"* Davutoğlu, 1998).

However, Fukuyama's piece and Davutoğlu's article were put under pressure with the publication of Samuel Huntington 1996 master piece *"The Clashes of Civilization and the Remaking of the World Order"*, in 1996 which predicted the confrontation between Communist and Capitalist ideologies, democracy and authoritarianism, dominant cultures and less dominant cultures, extreme religions and moderate religions. These clashes Huntington predicted. These clashes would cause sharp divisions and upheavals in socio-economic and political spheres.

So, the remaking of the world into the 'new world order' has been championed by US and European powers through the spread of third and four waves of democratization. These waves are being resisted by conservative Communist countries as well conservative capitalist States. Some of the capitalist States that went through the first and second waves of democratization are still resisting changes in ancient political systems. For example, the continued monarchy system in the UK and parts of Western Europe.

Now, we are living in such an accelerated flow of history, we cannot be static or harbour prejudices in our minds and stereotypes, if we want to understand this new global transformation. How should we address such a transformation? First of all, there is a need for political change. There is nothing like the Cold War - a Eurocentric or Euro-Atlantic plus the Soviet Union, centre of world politics any more. There are new rising powers, the language of politics has changed, as have the structures of politics and there is a need for a new response to this. For example, as a question, as a global order, the UN system is based on five permanent members who are able to decide on political issues for all of humanity. What is the legitimacy of having this structure? In the 1950s, 60s, 70s they had legitimacy because of wining Second World War. But now, the gap between the human conscience and political mechanisms of UN Security Council have widen. Which institution represents human consciousness in world politics? Is it the UN Security Council or General Assembly? The UN General Assembly is composed of 194 nations, while UN Security Council five permanent members and ten non-permanent members. Of course, if you look at the inclusiveness, UN General Assembly represents the general human conscience, while the UN Security Council represents operational capacity and efficiency and power politics. We need both. But at the end of the day, which one will prevail? The poor performance of these bodies represents the poor performance of humanity.

The 'new world order' is continued being installed through liberal democracy, human rights, and individualism and through globalization. Although the US sphere-headed these values, globalization has been taken up seriously by China challenging the current US administration to adopt it in full.

After 9/11 instead of liberty and democratization, the political paradigm shifted to increased security and more control. This is apparent in airports or other places that require security. Of course, world politics changed in response to the security challenge of terrorism. And that has affected cultural relations. The reign of the right wings such as Donald J. Trump as President of most powerful State on earth with his racist, misogynist and self-centred politics put the world into a dangerous place. However, after the winning of US presidential elections by Joe R. Biden, a true liberal, the political transformation of the world has begun in earnest. Nonetheless, the Russia-Ukraine war is risking the re-transformation of world order giving comparative politics scholars a lot to consider.

8.10. Arab Spring, Causes and Consequences

Arab springs, awakenings, uprisings or revolutions have been a great watershed in Middle East and North Africa (MENA) and global politics. This spontaneous transformation confined to the Arab world took a few days to create domino effect. in causing domino effect. For more than six years now, the Arab world has been the scene of epic paroxysm; the greatest wave of dissatisfaction the world had seen in the last twenty years. From the Atlantic to the Pacific, young people moved by decades of disappointments with their elites chose to unravel the dust of their disappointments and revolt against their governments. They shook the status quo, which has kept their situation miserable not only since their grandparents threw off the brutal yoke of colonialism with no improvement in economic, political, and social conditions.

The inciting event was the self-immolation of a street vendor, Mohamed El Bouazizi in Sidi Bouzid, Tunisia. This was a moment is one of psychological rupture between the populace and "the man on the horseback" who had promised to restore historical prestige, achieve national prosperity, and build a bright future (Fawaz, 2012). When Mohamed El Bouazizi committed his final act of desperate protest on December, 17th 2010, he was not aware that it would be the first in a long chain of events that claimed four of the regimes of the longest-sitting Arab leaders (Aissa, 2012).

However, leading up to the fall of those regimes, various changes had occurred that made the revolution possible. The two pillars of stability in Arab dictatorships – the military security complex and the state control over the economy – were shaken due to the civilians' revolutions. While the cases of the Tunisia and Egypt, Syria and Yemen to mention but a few were quite devastating, majority of Arab springs countries reacted with military against the civilians. However, allowing citizens' rights under the constitutions has always been crucial for solidification and longevity of the regimes in those polities.

Causes of the Arab Springs

Scholars of Middle Eastern and North African studies have underlined the causes of the Arab springs as economic recession, political dissatisfaction, corruption and demographics dimensions. However, the triggers were the use of various forms of media and the lack of education among the populace.

Media as a Powerful Tool in the Arab Spring

The uprisings in the Arab States have in common a wide and effective use of social media to communicate among themselves, mobilize their countrymen as well as to reach out to broadcasting channels and news media. The pictures of El Bouazizi at the Facebook page with the slogan "We are all Khalid Said" (Gardner, 2011) and the numerous slogans echoing that the people wanted to bring down the regime were transferred millions of times and impacted the outcome of the show of force between the regimes and their populations. When street protests grew and the miliary responded, the images of resulting violence were conveyed worldwide by multiple platforms. These images were crucial for the population's final victory.

However, the environment of the Arab Spring was also marked by highly influential cable media with a stark absence of the state media. Questions remain as to the role played by some media in stirring the masses and in some cases even breaching their own codes of conduct. Resignations of journalists, some of them long-established icons,

(Khanfar, 2011) speak of the climate surrounding the unethical actions of some Arab media in the unfolding of the Arab Spring episodes.

Role of Education in Shaping the Outbreak of the Uprising.

It is hard to assess which role the level of literacy played in the events; however, it is quite clear that the educational environment in the Arab world was ripe for the emergence of such upheavals. A 2009 background paper for the United Nations Educational, Scientific, and Cultural Organization (UNESCO) stated that while "low and perhaps deteriorating quality has been the major failing of Arab (public) education systems, private for-profit education has not helped improve quality of education significantly" (UNESCO Report, 2011). The same report pointed out that the scope of private provision of education has been growing ever since governments have been urged to withdraw from providing direct public services under structural adjustment policies.

Consequences of the Arab Spring

Infectious/Diffusion Effects and Overthrowing of Leaders as follows

- **Tunisia**: President Zine El Abidine Ben Ali was ousted, charged, exiled and the government overthrown.
- **Egypt**: President Hosni Mubarak was ousted, arrested, charged, and the government overthrown.
- **Libya**: Leader Muammar Gaddafi was killed following a civil war that saw a foreign military intervention, and the government overthrown.
- **Yemen**: President Ali Abdullah Saleh was ousted, and power was handed to a national unity government.
- **Syria**: President Bashar al-Assad faces a civil uprising against his rule that deteriorates into armed rebellion and eventual full-scale civil war.
- **Bahrain**: Civil uprising against the government crushed by authorities and Saudi-led intervention.

- **Kuwait, Lebanon and Oman**: Government changes implemented in response to protests.
- **Morocco and Jordan**: Constitutional reforms implemented in response to protests.
- **Saudi Arabia, Sudan, Mauritania, and other Arab countries**: Protests and changes of leadership.

Iran, Saudi Arabia and Turkey's Strategic Games

Seeking to fill the power vacuum created by these changes. Tehran, Riyadh and Ankara participated in a three-way competition for resources and position. This triangular relation is shaping the future security design of the region including Syria (Naimi, 2012). What is puzzling about this situation is that the US seems to be at best only playing a supporting role instead of taking the lead. The US Administration, which has been in a reactive mode thus far, seems to be watching a Turkish-Saudi ad-hoc coalition designed to contain Iran activities in Syria after Teheran's success in Iraq conflicts and its strategic games in Bahrain. And while it has been unable to break the traditional support given by China and Russia to the Islamic Republic, the US is keeping a low profile on the humanitarian issues in Gulf countries and not interfering with Ankara's planning with regards to Syria, even though Turkey 's stance on Syria may trigger an open conflict with Iran (Duman, 2017).

The Arab People as a New Actor

In the Arab world, the populations have never been really involved in the process of choosing their rulers or in sharing the dividends of wealth, let alone participating in the decision-making process of their countries.

Indeed, it was obvious by the end of December 2010 that some of the Arab regimes had blurred the line between the status of a republic and a monarchy. Months before the outbreak of the revolutions,

Egypt, Libya, and Yemen were already flirting with Syria's example of a king like power transfer; a choice that Western chancelleries seemed ready to accept for the sake of social stability and an expedient Global War on Terror (GWOT). On the other hand, the billions of dollars of frozen assets accumulated by the dictators and their inner circles speak to the decades of undistributed wealth and money embezzlement, the heavy cost of which was borne by the populations. Experts estimated Gaddafi's savings and investments at over $250 billion; all were hoarded in secret funds while many of his people were living under abject poverty (Duman, 2017).

The 2011 social uprisings were a culmination point for the tumultuous relationship Arab populations have always had with their rulers. Indeed, over the years, the Arab street metaphor coined by the Western media has become a buzzword that usually depicts Arab public opinion in a "negatively framed and sui generis fashion" (Regier & Khalidi, 2009). This refers to anger Arab public went through.

The Rise of the Islamists
The second set of new actors to emerge on the stage is the Islamists. Though not fatal in itself, the arrival of Islamist-led governments is being closely watched. What would be the outcome of an Arab League Summit should the Cairo-based organization serve as a tribune for vociferous leaders to reach out to enflamed populations? What if these governments grow more responsive and yield to the populations' demands by opening their borders, especially in support of regional causes? What might be the result of an Islamic Summit held in 1997 to garner support for the Iranian regime? These are some of the uncertainties that foreign stakeholders might need to consider while dealing with the region.

Potential End of the Anti-Americanism Feeling

While disenfranchised Arab populations may continue to serve as a fertile ground for terrorist recruiting, it seems highly unlikely that a free, rehabilitated Arab society would continue to blame American interventionism or support of oppressive regimes for its political, economic and social failures. In this regard, the US administration can build on the fact that the Arab springs was not only a counter jihad trend among the Sunni Muslims more than 80 percent of Islamic world but also a rejection of the Islamic ideology which automatically sees itself at odds with the West (Wright, 2011). Such an understanding benefited the Obama administration which scored credible points since it has vowed to follow a smart power foreign policy in the region (Clinton, 2009).

However, the United States as a global power may still be seen through the lens of the role it pledges to play in solving the Arab-Israeli conflict. According to the Zogby International poll of Arab public opinion conducted in key American allied countries in the region, confirmed a consistency in the Arab street showing that the respondents consider the "continuing occupation of Palestinian lands" as "the greatest obstacle to peace and stability in the Middle East" (Furia & Lucas, 2006). Therefore, it will be up to the American Administration to seize the opportunity of the regime change in the region to give a new start to the peace process.

Arab spring can be understood from the following arguments: Which end-state in the MENA region?

The most important thing about the Arab Spring perhaps is that the stone is still rolling. Even though elections have brought some hope to the populations, the processes engaged so far have shown little progress and the future of the region remains bleak. The Egyptian experience seems to require more time before being confirmed as successful. The case of Libya with foreign military intervention has not brought hoped for. This should be taken into consideration before striking a hasty analogy between Syria and Libya.

Façade Democratization

Arab Springers hope that democratization was going to be the result of the Arab uprising. Daniel Brumberg (2002) puts it best in his article: *"Democratization in the Arab World? The Trap of Liberalized Autocracy:"* argues:

> "Because (Arab regimes) have failed to create a robust political society in which non-Islamists can secure the kind of organized popular support that Islamists command, these hybrid regimes have created circumstances under which free elections could well make illiberal Islamist the dominant opposition voice, leaving democrats (whether secularist or Islamist) caught between ruling autocrats and Islamist would be-autocrats. Hence the great dilemma in which substantive democratization and genuine pluralism become at once more urgently needed and more gravely risky. Indeed, Arab Spring did not democratize Arab world" (Brumberg, 2002).

However, the Arab Spring fully established moderate, non-violent, and citizen-focused political Islam, as opposed to fanatic ideological Islamism. The elections held so far and the premises from Libya and even Syria, should there be a regime change in the foreseeable future, reinforce that democratization is not far from the Arab world/MENA. Nonetheless, Arab spring has been a failure in many situations, case in point is Libya which has remained ungovernable state.

8.11. Democracy, Durable Authoritarianism, or Incomplete Transitions

The troubling impression created by political events in durable authoritarian and incomplete transition States is supported by the latest findings of the *Freedom in the World group, 2021*. A total of 67 countries suffered net declines in political rights and civil liberties (durable authoritarianism and incomplete transitions) in 2020, compared with 36 that registered gains in 2021 (Puddington & Roylance, 2021). This marked the 13th consecutive year in which declines outnumbered improvements.

While in past years the declines in democracy were generally concentrated among autocracies and dictatorships that simply went from bad to worse. In 2021, it was established that democracies that were rated free in the world ranking report were systematically declining and got serious governance setbacks. In fact, free countries accounted for a larger share of the countries with declines than at any time in the past decade, and nearly one-quarter of the countries registering declines in 2021 were in Europe.

Table 2: Worst Durable Authoritarian and Incomplete Transition Countries

Of the 51 countries designated as Not Free, the following 11 have the worst aggregate scores for political rights and civil liberties (durable authoritarian and incomplete transiting countries).

Country/Territory	Aggregate Score (out of 100)
South Sudan	-1
Syria	-1
Eritrea	2

North Korea	2
Uzbekistan	3
Turkmenistan	3
Somalia	3
Sudan	4
Equatorial Guinea	6
Central African Republic	6
Saudi Arabia	7

Source: Freedom House Report, 2022

As the year drew to a conclusion, the major democracies were mired in anxiety and indecision after a series of destabilizing events. In the United States, the presidential victory of Donald Trump, a mercurial figure with unconventional views on foreign policy and other matters, raised questions about the country's future role in the world. Britain's vote to leave the European Union, the collapse of the Italian government after a failed referendum on constitutional reform, a series of antidemocratic moves by the new government in Poland, and gains by xenophobic nationalist parties elsewhere in Europe similarly cast doubt on the strength of the alliances that shaped the institutions of global democracy.

At the same time, Russia, in stunning displays of hubris and hostility, interfered in the political processes of the United States and other democracies, escalated its military support for the Assad dictatorship in Syria, and continued its illegal occupation of Ukrainian territory. China also flouted international law, ignoring a tribunal's ruling against its expansive claims of sovereignty over the South China Sea and intensifying its repression of dissent within its borders. And unscrupulous leaders from South Sudan and Ethiopia to Thailand and the Philippines engaged in human rights violations of varying scales with impunity.

In the wake of developments in 2022, it is no longer possible to speak with confidence about the long-term durability of the EU; the incorporation of democracy and human rights priorities into American foreign policy; the resilience of democratic institutions in Central Europe, Brazil, or South Africa; or even the expectation that actions like the assault on Myanmar's Rohingya minority or indiscriminate bombing in Yemen will draw international criticism from democratic governments and UN human rights bodies. No such assumption, it seems, is entirely safe.

Freedom in the World: 2022 Trend Arrows

The year 2022 was characterized by the erosion of democratic institutions, and left few positive trends to highlight. Of the 11 countries that received trend arrows calling special attention to developments of major significance, only one denotes improvement.

Colombia — Colombia received an upward trend arrow due to the peace process between the government and left-wing FARC guerrillas, leading to a reduction in violence.

China — China's downward trend arrow reflects the chilling effect generated by cyber security and foreign NGO laws, increased internet surveillance, and lengthy prison sentences for human rights lawyers, activists, and religious believers.

Ethiopia — Ethiopia received a downward trend arrow due to security forces' disproportionate and often violent response to primarily peaceful antigovernment protests.

Hong Kong — Hong Kong's downward trend arrow reflects Beijing's encroachment on freedoms in the territory and the central government's unilateral reinterpretation of the Basic Law.

Mozambique — Mozambique experienced an increase in political tensions and violence, including the abuse of civilian populations by security forces.

Nicaragua — Nicaragua received a downward trend arrow due to the expulsion of opposition leaders and lawmakers, plus government efforts to silence journalists and academics.

Philippines — Philippines received a downward trend arrow due to the thousands of extrajudicial killings carried out as part of newly elected president Rodrigo Duterte's war on drugs.

Poland — Poland's downward trend arrow reflects sustained attempts by the ruling Law and Justice party to increase government influence over the media, judiciary, civil service, and education system.

South Sudan — South Sudan received a downward trend arrow due to the slow implementation of a peace deal, the resumption of violence across the states and egregious human rights abuses against citizens by government forces and others.

Turkey — Turkey received a downward trend arrow due to the security and political repercussions of the July 2016 coup attempt, which led to mass arrests and firings of civil servants and other perceived enemies.

Zambia — Zambia's downward trend arrow reflects the restrictive environment for the political opposition in the run-up to general elections.

Source: Freedom House Report 2022

Syria's Impact on Democracies

While the democratic world stood aside throughout the year, a coalition of repressive dictatorships bombed and shelled Aleppo and other Syrian cities where opponents of President Bashar al-Assad had gained footholds. Assad, with crucial assistance from Russia, Iran, and a multinational array of Iranian-backed Shiite militias, clearly regained the initiative in the five-year civil war, whose grinding violence has killed hundreds of thousands of people and displaced millions more (**Puddington & Roylance, 2021**). A US-led coalition pounded the Islamic State (IS) militant group in the east but left the pro-Assad alliance undisturbed as it focused its military might on non-IS rebels and civilians.

Since the war began, each new horror has appeared to deter rather than motivate a coordinated international response. The conflict has only grown more complex and intractable, however, and democratic governments continue to reap the consequences of their hesitation.

The enormous refugee flows and IS-inspired terrorism generated by the Syrian conflicts have played an important role in the weakening of democratic standards in Europe and the United States. Arrivals of asylum seekers in Europe declined in 2016, largely due to the hardening of borders in the Balkans and an agreement between the EU and Turkey in which Ankara pledged to block irregular departures. But the drop in numbers failed to stem anti-refugee rhetoric, as European political leaders routinely smeared those fleeing conflict zones as criminals, rapists, and terrorists (Brumberg, 2002).

Moreover, the agreement with Turkey—an already dubious haven for refugees given its raging Kurdish insurgency and regular terrorist attacks—became a deeper source of embarrassment after Turkish President Recep Tayyip Erdoğan embraced an unvarnished form of authoritarianism in response to a failed coup attempt in July 2016. Having put down the coup, the government-imposed emergency rule that resulted in the arrest of nearly 52,000 civilians, the imprisonment of dozens of journalists, the shuttering of hundreds of media outlets and nongovernmental organizations (NGOs), the arrest of the leaders and hundreds of officials from the third-largest party in the parliament, and the firing of more than a hundred thousand civil servants.

Terrorism continued to fuel political upheaval in Europe and the United States despite major territorial losses suffered by IS and other extremist groups such as Boko Haram. France, Belgium, and Germany endured high-profile terrorist attacks, an IS-inspired mass shooting struck the US state of Florida, and smaller assaults elsewhere in Europe were foiled or interrupted by the authorities.

Several European governments reacted by adopting laws that gave enhanced powers to security forces and eased constraints on surveillance. More ominously, persistent fears over the upsurge in terrorist attacks stoked public hostility toward Muslim minorities and immigrants, deepening existing social rifts and threatening civil liberties. During the American presidential campaign, Donald Trump at various times promised to prevent all Muslims from entering the United States, deport Syrians already in the country, and carry out "extreme vetting" of the beliefs of refugees and immigrants. Joe Biden has different view which is quite liberal in nature that regulates the immigration equally for all Americans and the immigrants of the United States.

Radicalizing Authoritarian States

The conflicts in the Middle East and political upheavals in the democracies often deflected the world's attention from worsening domestic repression in China, Russia, and other authoritarian countries, which stand to gain from a breakdown in democratic norms at the international level. In fact, both Beijing and Moscow stepped up efforts to reshape the world in their own image.

In China, the Communist Party regime led by President Xi Jinping tightened its grip with the adoption of new laws and regulations on cyber security, foreign nonprofits, and religious affairs. Heavy sentences handed down to human rights lawyers, microbloggers, grassroots activists, and religious believers dealt an additional blow to those seeking to improve conditions in the country.

As Xi Jing Ping consolidated his personal power, moving rapidly away from the existing pattern of collective leadership within the party elite, he sought to enforce greater ideological discipline through a propaganda campaign that forbade intraparty dissent and relentlessly criticized "Western" democratic values. The regime also advanced plans to introduce a "social credit" system that would connect each citizen's financial, social, political, and legal data to produce a single numerical rating of his or her behavior and trustworthiness. A misstep in one area would presumably have repercussions in every other aspect of an individual's life.

Beijing's growing intolerance for individual autonomy at home was mirrored by its intrusions into the affairs of neighboring societies. The leadership issued an unprecedented ruling on Hong Kong's Basic Law with the aim of preventing pro-independence and pro-democracy politicians from taking their seats in the self-governing territory's legislature. The Chinese government similarly adopted a hostile attitude toward Taiwan after the local opposition party, which opposes unification with China, swept to victory in presidential and parliamentary elections. And Beijing has intensified its pressure on governments in the region to return those who have fled China to escape persecution, especially members of the Uighur Muslim minority.

Russia followed a comparable pattern, combining domestic repression with an ambitious program of regional intimidation and long-distance political sabotage. The regime of President Vladimir Putin stage-managed Russia's parliamentary and regional elections, leading to record low turnout and the total extinction of liberal opposition in the legislature. The Kremlin also added to its blacklists of "extremist" websites and NGOs that it considers "foreign agents" or "undesirable" to its blacklist of "extremist" websites and NGOs.

Outside its borders, Russia radically accelerated its indiscriminate bombing campaign against population centers held by anti-Assad rebels in Syria, contributing little to the fight against IS elsewhere in the country. Moscow also deepened its interference in elections in established democracies through a strategy that combined support for populist and nationalist parties, theft and publication of the internal documents of mainstream parties and candidates, and the aggressive dissemination of fake news and propaganda. Russia's efforts to influence the Italian constitutional referendum and the presidential election in the United States represented a major leap forward in Putin's bid to undermine the integrity and even change the outcome of democratic processes.

Orphan Democrats

Citizens in many vulnerable democracies such as Taiwan and the Baltic states, are alert to durable authoritarian threats. Others in places like, North Korea, Hong Kong, Tunisia, and Ukraine understand that the survival of their democracy depends on international democratic solidarity. Protesters, activists, refugees, and besieged civilians around the world rely on the promise of international aid and advocacy backed up by democratic governments.

The question is whether the United States and Europe will ignore their own long-term interests and retreat from their responsibilities as global leaders. If they do, Russia, China and Iran can be expected to fill the void.

CHAPTER NINE

Comparative Ethnic Politics and National Identity

9.1. The Concept of Ethnicity

Ethnicity as a term designates a sense of collective belonging, which could be based on common descent, language, history, culture, race or religion (or some combination of these (Horowitz, 1985). Some would like to separate religion from this list, letting ethnicity incorporate the other attributes.

Ethnicity is a complex concept to be defined. Many scholars continued to contest the definition of ethnicity. For example, a neo-liberal scholar, Philips Mair who is a social scientist views an ethnic group as a people sharing the same historical experience, having the same culture, speaking the same language and sharing the belief about the future together (Mair, 1992). Other neo-liberal theorists such as Zolberg (1998) and Young (1999) view ethnicity as an inevitable consequence of modernization, economic development and political development, especially in Africa. The neo-liberal theorists believe that an ethnic group has as its members, people who share a conviction that they have common interests and fate, and they tend to propound a cultural symbolism expressing their cohesiveness. Ethnic groups differ from other groups in their composition because they include persons from every stage of life and social class. It is viewed that the insignia of ethnicity is inescapable. Nelson Kasfir (1976) suggests four ways of recognizing ethnic groups. These are (i) culture; (ii) language; (iii) traditional political organization; and (iv) territoriality. Succinctly, members of an ethnic group must share a common culture, language and custom and occupy the same territory (Kasfir, 1976).

According to Okwudiba Nnoli (2007), ethnicity is a very complex phenomenon. It is always closely associated with political, economic, social, religious and other social views and interactions (Nnoli, 2007). Hence ethnicity finds expression in political domination, economic exploitation, psychological oppression and class manipulation. Perhaps the commonest explanation of what an ethnic group means is that which says that it comprises of people with a common ancestry. In other words, this refers to people who can trace their pedigrees to one ancestor. Apparently, most definitions and explanations of the term, by social and political scientists, seem to draw from this perspective. Max Weber (1968) for instance, described the ethnic group as "those human groups that entertain a subjective belief in their common descent" (Kasfir, 1976). The main elements of ethnicity according to Nnoli (2007) include "exclusiveness manifested in inter-group competition, conflict in relation to stiff competition, and the consciousness of being one in relation to others" (Nnoli, 2007).

In addition to these, Mair (1992) identifies three main characteristics of ethnicity:

> "One, it is a culturally specific practice and unique set
> of symbols and beliefs, especially the way in which an
> ascribed identity is given contemporary construction
> through socialization and mobilization in cultural and
> political movements. Two, it is a belief in common origin
> involving sometimes, the existence or imagination of a
> common past. Third and finally, it involves a sense of

belonging to a group defined in opposition to others"
(Mair, 1992).

A critical examination of these three elements on which ethnic
identity rests shows an attempt to bridge the gap in literature between
those who take ethnicity as a primordial inheritance and those who
see it as something that is historically or socially constructed. Indeed,
there is an increasing tendency to discard the earliest approaches to
the conceptualization of ethnicity. These include approaches which
had emphasized ethnicity as primordial (Geertz, 1963) and those that
present ethnicity as a handover of the past which modernization –
access to the media, western education and urbanization are expected
to whittle down in the course of time.

9.2. The Concept of Ethnic Politics

It is quite perturbing getting to review scholarly definitions of ethnic
politics as it has been highly contested by political scientists and political practitioners. However, career politicians seemed to have preferred
definitions. Thus, ethnic politics is defined as *"politics that's based solely
on a tribe and ethnicity and that's doomed to tear a country apart, it's a
failure, a failure of imagination" (Obama, 2008).*

Our theory of ethnic politics and conflict is based on two pillars.
First, we rely on institutionalist theories that show how established
structures of political legitimacy provide incentives for actors to
pursue certain types of political strategies. Second, our model
follows a configurationally logic. Depending on the configuration
of political power, similar political institutions can produce different
consequences, while similar consequences can result from different
constellations of power. The institutionalist part of the argument
specifies the conditions under which political loyalties will align along
ethnic cleavages; the configurationally part explains when we expect

such ethnic politics to lead to armed violence and how it should return to genuine peace.

9.3. Institutional Incentives for Ethnic Politics

We derive the institutionalist part of the argument from Andreas Wimmer's (2013), theory of nation-state formation and ethnic politics. It states that ethnicity matters for politics, not because of a universal, naturally-given tendency to favour (ethnic) kin over non-kin (as socio-biologists argue), nor because of a primordial attachment of individuals to their identities, nor because it provides lower costs for political organizations (as the political economy tradition maintains) (Wimmer, 2013). Rather, ethnicity matters because the nation-state itself relies on ethno-national principles of political legitimacy: the state is ruled in the name of an ethnically defined people and rulers should therefore care for "their own people" (Wimmer, 2013). As a result, ethnicity and nationhood have much greater political significance in nation-states than they do in other types of polities such as empires or city-states. Given this institutional environment, political office holders have incentives to gain legitimacy by favouring co-ethnics or co-nationals over others when distributing public goods and government jobs; judiciary bodies have incentives to apply the principle of equality before the law more for co-ethnics or co-nationals than for others; the police have incentives to provide protection for co-ethnics or co-nationals, but less for others; and so forth. The expectation of ethnic preference and discrimination works the other way too. Voters prefer parties led by co-ethnics or co-nationals, delinquents hope for co-ethnic or co-national judges, and citizens prefer to be policed by co-ethnics or co-nationals. Not all modern nation-states are characterized by such ethnic and national favouritism.

As we discuss elsewhere, this favouritism is more likely in poor states that lack the resources for universal inclusion, as well as in states with weak civil society institutions where other, nonethnic channels for aggregating political interests and rewarding political loyalty are scarce (Wimmer, 2013). In such states, political leaders and followers orient their strategies toward avoiding dominance by ethnic or national. Others they strive for the self-determination and self-rule that are at the core of nationalist ideology. This motive is at the same time material, political, and symbolic: "adequate" or "just" representation in a central government offers material advantages, such as access to government jobs and services; legal advantages such as the benefits of full citizenship rights, a fair trial, and protection from arbitrary violence; and symbolic advantages such as the prestige of belonging to a "state-owning" ethnic or national group. The aggregate consequence of these strategic orientations is a struggle over control of the state between ethnically defined actors or ethnic politics for short (Rothschild, 1981). Such ethnic politics may lead to a process of political mobilization, counter-mobilization, and escalation. Political leaders appeal to the ideal of self-rule and fair representation enshrined in the nation-state model to mobilize their followers against the threat of ethnic dominance by others. These demands may stir the fear of ethnic dominance among other political elites and their ethnic constituencies and result in a process of counter-mobilization. The conflicting demands may finally spiral into armed confrontation. The argument of institutional incentives does not explicitly address the logic of this escalation process but seeks to specify the ethno-political configurations that make it more likely.

9.4. The Concepts of National Identity, Taxonomies and Ethnicity as Primordial Attachment

The ambiguity and controversy surrounding the discourse of the concepts of identity in social sciences is indeed baffling (Brubaker, 2002, Brubaker & Cooper, 2000; Voros, 2006). The scholarship on identity is therefore highly divided. Broadly, three schools of thought or models are discerned. These are primordialism (scholars associated with this school are Edward Shilts, Clifford Geertz, Piere Van De Berghe), Constructivism (Ernest, Gellner, Benedict Anderson, Eric Hobsbawm, John Breuilly, Paul R. Brass) and Ethno-symbolism (Smith, 2009).

Further as derivatives, two main conceptual and theoretical models dealing with national identity are also duly identified. These are the civic and the ethnic. The schools/theories are further identified as modernist/constructivist/instrumentalist, on the one hand and primordialist/essentialist/intrinsic, on the other (Brubaker, 2006). The modernist/ constructivist/instrumentalist cluster has for several decades now, particularly in sociology, political science and political anthropology, assumed the dominant model of identity analysis and theorizing (Voros, 2006).

Firstly, according to the ethnicist or primordialist model (henceforth primordialist), the set of the dichotomy, identity is perceived as a repository of collective memory, a manifestation of imagination that could assume various contours. The collective memory, in turn, is presumably spawned by constitutive variables such as descent, blood ties, linguistic affiliation, homestead, kinship, etc. The primordialist model distinguishes itself through reposting identity at the ethnic social store whose contours invariably may be real or imaginary common descent, shared speech, common cultural traits, defining specific or unique commonality (Connor, 1994).

Identity has increasingly come to be conflated (Bereketeab, 2012). While driven by the politics of identity, identity itself is heading toward fragmentation, seeking to lift up the constituent units as separate and independent, the result of which is a proliferation of identities. Will Kymlicka (1995), argues that the most liberal theorists have recognized identity as an expression of one's membership in a political community (Kymlicka, 1995). In this conceptualization of membership, an individual could be a member of (a) political community (national), and (b) of a cultural community (sub-national). Though membership in one of these social categories the individual has rights and duties that are inherent characters of identity.

Secondly, the civic or modernist model, on the other hand, locates identity at the civic repository premises whose contours are invariably identified as territoriality, residence under common secular law, loyalty to and identifying with common national symbols (flag, national holidays, buildings, etc), national institutions such as parliament, judiciary, loyalty to an overarching state (Anderson, 1991). The civic/modernist model, broadly understood as characterizing modern identity, is therefore related to the modern state, that is, allegiance to the state.

The third school of thought or model, ethno-symbolism, rejects the premises of both primordialism and constructivism and concludes that there is a continuation between the two. It argues that primordial identity is transformed into the modern one. Unlike the primordialist that claims that identity is perennial, or the modernist who claims it is a modern construction, the ethno-symbolist traces continuity and change (Armstrong, 2017; Hutchinson, 2000).

Recently another school/model that rejects constructivism, or rather deconstructs it, has emerged, notably the post-modernist. While constructivism in its analysis of identity pursues methodological nationalism, deconstructivism pursues methodological cosmopolitanism. In the case of the former, the unit of analysis is the collective (nation), whereas in the case of the latter, the unit of analysis is the individual (Bereketeab, 2012). For the post-modernist, identity is cosmopolitan, transnational, cross-cultural, trans-territorial, global etc (Clark, 2009).

Whereas identity for the primordialist is given, natural, constant and incontestable, for the modernist, it is malleable, constructed, conditional, contestable, narrative-based and susceptible to cultural and environmental impacts (Lustick et al, 2004). For the post-modernist school, identity is deconstructed, de-narrated, formless and shapeless,

Table 3: Concepts and Theories of Identity

Variable	Primordial Communalism	Ethno-Symbolism	Modernism Constructivism	Post-Modernism Deconstructivism
Identity	Ethnic Community Sub-nationalism	Ethnie	Civic Collective Nation	Civic Individual Post-Nation State
Methodology	Methodological Communalism		Methodological Nationalism National	Methodological Cosmopolitanism Regional
Ethnic Politics		.		

situational and inter-subjective; indeed, it only exists in the interlocutory space of individuals.

9.5. Political Salience of Sectarian Divisions, Political Competition and Ethnic Mobilization

Sectarianism is a rule by religious fanatics, pitting one religion against another (Sham, 2016). In many countries, particularly, in a state where religion is a very sharp cleavage, sectarian divisions are quite strong. The majority of Middle East countries, particularly, Muslim-dominated are sectarian States. They include Iraq, Iran, Lebanon, Saudi Arabia, Yemen, Kuwait, Bahrian, Pakistan, Afghanistan, Azerbaijan, Syria etc. In Sub-Saharan Africa, we have Nigeria, Central Africa Republic (CAR), Sudan, and Somalia etc. However, in this book, our focus shall be mostly on Middle East countries due to the salience of sectarian politics and divisions.

Political Competition and Ethnic Mobilization

There are at least three schools of thought in the social sciences that explain ethno-nationalist mobilization and these we explained as: primordialism, instrumentalism and constructivism. They are useful in explaining the rise of religious sectarianism and political mobilization in Muslim societies given that most mainstream forms of politicized Islam are religious forms of nationalism whose actors have accepted the borders of the post-colonial state and are fundamentally concerned with the internal national politics of their home countries. Moreover, Muslim sectarian discourses of power and their underlying paradigm of politics are "ethnic" in the sense they are concerned with the politics of group identity where the group in question self-identifies with religion as a key marker of its identity. Furthermore, as Harvard scholar, David Little (2017) argued "there are several other ways in which ethnicity and religion are connected" (Little, 2017). In his survey and analysis of nationalist conflicts, he observes that there "is a widespread tendency of ethnic groups in all cultural contexts to authenticate themselves religiously that lends plausibility to the term, 'ethnoreligious" (Ibid). He goes on to note that in particular cases "it is artificial to try to distinguish too sharply between religious and non-religious ethnic attributes" (Ibid). In those instances where religious identity becomes ethnically salient, language, customs, even genealogy, take on strongly religious overtones" (Ibid). This suggests that functionally speaking, ethnicity and religion are deeply intertwined and often overlap and mutually reinforce each other. Aspects of the Sunni-Shi'a divide, particularly between Iranian Shi'a and Arab Sunnis, support this view thus giving credence to the utilization of the social scientific literature on nationalism and ethnic politics in assessing religious sectarianism and conflict in Muslim societies today. Apart from Muslims in Middle East, the rise of ethnoreligious tensions has also occurred in other religious societies. This has been seen with a rise of religious divisions and tensions in Jonglei state fitting Bishop Moses Anur Ayom and Ruben Akurdit Ngong of Bor Diocese over the contest of Jonglei Internal Province.

Returning to the three schools of thought on what we can now call "ethno-religious," the first school, primordialism views ethnicity as a shared sense of group identity that is natural and deeply embedded in social relations and human psychology. For primordialists, ethnicity is based on a set of intangible elements rooted in biology, history and tradition that tie an individual to a larger collective. Ethnic mobilization is tied to emotional and often irrational notions of group solidarity and support (Smith, 2009). In societies, where other forms of social solidarity around gender, labour or class are weak, ethnoreligious mobilization is often an integral part of political life. One of the major criticisms leveled at primordialism is that it does not explicate the link between identity and conflict. While primordialism has utility in identifying where ethnic ties are prevalent, it does not tell us how it can be a factor in mobilizing identity during times of conflict. The existence of multiple identities among social actors suggests that they are often manipulated as part of a mobilization process into cause-and-effect scenarios (Tiemessen, 2005). Instrumentalism, by contrast, suggests that ethnicity is malleable and is defined as part of a political process. The idea of manipulation is thus an inherent part of this school of thought. By emphasizing in-group similarities and out-group differences as well as invoking the fear of assimilation, domination or annihilation, ethno-religious leaders can stimulate identity mobilization (Fearon & Laitin, 1996). For instrumentalists, ethnic mobilization is a by-product of the personal political projects of leaders and elites who are interested in advancing their political and economic interests via social conflict. Placed within a larger context of conflict escalation, instrumentalism allows us to make cross-comparisons between societies with similar social cleavages.

Constructivism adopts a middle ground between primordialism and instrumentalism. Its proponents argue that ethnicity is not fixed but rather a political construct based on a dense web of social relationships (Anderson, 1993). Like primordialists, constructivists recognize the importance of seemingly immutable features of ethnic/religious identity but they disagree that this inevitably leads to conflict. On the other hand, constructivists share with instrumentalists the view that elites and leadership play a critical role in the mobilization process; disagreement emerges, however, on the degree to which these identities can be manipulated. In brief, constructivists do not believe that ethnicity/religion is inherently conflictual but rather conflict flows from "pathological social systems" and "political opportunity structures" that breed conflict from many social cleavages and which are beyond the control of the individual (Rothschild, 1981).

Middle East Context and Genesis of Sectarian Divisions

While most Muslim-majority, societies are Sunni, constituting about 90 percent of the total global Muslim population, Iran, Iraq, Azerbaijan and Bahrain are Shi'a-majority societies. Significant Shi'a populations also live in Lebanon, Afghanistan, Kuwait, Yemen, Saudi Arabia, Pakistan and Syria. Critically, what these societies share in common is that most of their political systems are decidedly non-democratic and various forms of authoritarianism dominate the political landscape. It is this overarching fact that determines the ebb and flow of political life and influences the relationship between sects, the rise of sectarianism and the behaviour of political and religious leaders. Authoritarian states in the Muslim world have several distinguishing features which influence sectarian relations. They suffer from a crisis of legitimacy and as a result they closely monitor and attempt to control civil society by limiting access to information and the freedom of association of their citizens. Joel Migdal (1988)'s concept of a "weak state" best describes these regimes (Migdal, 1988). In his formulation, based on an innovative model of state-society relations, "weak states" suffer from limited power and capacity to exert social control. They often cannot and do not control sections of the country both within urban and rural areas, over which they claim sovereignty. Moreover, they confront highly complex societies made up of a "mélange of social organizations" such as ethnic and religious groups, villages, landlords, clans, and various economic interest groups which limit the state's reach into society and compromise its autonomy. Dispersed domination, the state (any other social force) managed to achieve its full autonomy (Ibid). While the state is too weak to dominate society, it is often strong enough to manipulate and effectively respond to crises that threaten national security and regime survival (Nasr, 2000).

In weak states, politics revolves around strategies of survival. state leaders and political elites are fundamentally concerned with both their staying on power and staying in power. Thwarting rivals who might threaten them both from within society and among various state organizations is a key political obsession that drives and informs political decisions. A common tactic to preserve and perpetuate political rule in a weak state is to manipulate social and political cleavages via a divide-and rule-strategy. This gives ruling elites greater room to manoeuvre in the short term but often at the cost of social cohesion in the long term. This dominant feature of the politics of weak states also suggests why "state actors are principal agents in identity mobilization and conflict in culturally plural societies, and the manner in which politics of identity unfolds in a weak state is a product of the dialectic of state-society relations" (Nasr, 2000). Weak states, therefore, are more prone to sectarianism given that manipulating cleavages of identity is a dominant feature of their politics or as David Little has observed in his analysis of religion, nationalism and intolerance, "authoritarian states appear to draw life from ethnic or religious intolerance as a way of justifying the degree of violence required to maintain (and perpetuate) power" (Little, 2017).

During the 1960s and 1970s, in several Muslim countries, political opposition to the ruling regimes was in the form of various socialist, communist and left-wing political formations. In an attempt to pacify these oppositional currents, Islamic political groups were allowed greater freedom of movement and association in the hope that they would challenge the popularity of these secular oppositional groups thus immunizing the state from criticism and scrutiny. The most dramatic case of this was in Egypt when Anwar Sadat released scores of Muslim Brotherhood members from jail and allowed exile leaders to return home. This was a watershed period in the history of Egypt. Similarly, in an attempt to enhance the capacity of the Pakistani state and solidify political control, General Muhammad Zia Ul-Haqq launched an Islamization program in the late 1970s, which despite its pretensions to Islamic universalism was in essence an attempt at the Sunnification of political and social life of Pakistan. This was therefore viewed as a threat by religious minorities in Pakistan, the Shi'a community in particular, who considered these policies detrimental to their socio-political interests. The severe rupture in sectarian relations in Pakistan that soon followed was significantly shaped by this develop-ment but as Vali Nasr has demonstrated it was also deeply influenced by regional and international variables as well (Nasr, 2000).

9.6. Ethnicity, Social Class and Contentious Politics

Social class is defined through both structural and processual approaches, whereby the former interprets class as a matrix of fixed categories in which individuals move up or down a continuum while the latter interprets class as group identities shaped by common, shared experiences (Wright & Shin, 1988). Structural approaches to class analysis typically measure social class through indicators of socio-economic status such as income, occupation, and education. Marx Weber (1947) categorized classes as working class, lower middle class, intelligentsia, and upper class (Weber, 1947). Similar to Weber, the strat-ification of classes demonstrated through Warner's class model (1949) divides classes into upper, middle, and lower, with subdivisions in each (upper-upper class, lower upper class, upper-middle class, lower-middle class, upper-lower class, lower-lower class) (Warner, 1949). Newer varia-tions of Warner's model have since been produced by sociologists such as Gilbert (2002) and Thompson and Hickey (2005), and although the variations use different labels, the six hierarchical levels usually remain intact (Ibid). In comparison, processual approaches to class analysis explore how individuals develop, interpret, and display class identities.

While processual approaches have tremendous value in class anal-ysis, structural approaches are more appropriate to examine mobility. Mobility is broadly defined as the opportunity for one generation to increase relative earnings above the previous generation (Thompson and Hickey, 2005). The degree of mobility is often influenced by the opportunities available from one generation to the next. Advances in opportunity can be achieved through structural mobility, circula-tion mobility and ethnic favours. Nathan Bok (1996) defines structural mobility as the product of economic growth, which involves an increase in the total supply of opportunities (Bok, 1996). In comparison, circulation mobility is defined as a matter of how fairly society distributes the opportunities that already exist (Ibid).

Ethnicity plays a critical role in social class formations and mobility. Leaders in power would tend to favour members of their ethnic groups in resources and power allocations. This is out of fear that members of their ethnicity would help them to stay in power forever. Leaning toward ethnic extraction is a common belief of leaders in Sub-Saharan Africa (Chol, 2021). This always affects social class mobility given it is not totally based on meritocracy. Efforts to eschew ethnicity in social formation and class mobility have not achieved much in the sub-continent of Africa. It is Rwanda that has constitutionally endeavoured to shun away ethnicity consideration and favours in social, economic and political power and resources allocation in the government. Rwanda has indeed promoted meritocracy in the government.

On the other hand, contentious politics is the use of disruptive techniques to make a political point, or to change government policy. Examples of such techniques are actions that disturb the normal activities of societies such as riots, general strike action, demonstrations, terrorism, civil disobedience, and even revolution or social movement which often engage in contentious politics. Historical sociologist Charles Tilly (2008) defines contentious politics as "interactions in which actors make claims bearing on someone else's interest, in which governments appear either as targets, initiators of claims, or third parties" (Tilly, 2008).

Contentious politics centers on consequential collective claims: calls for action on the part of some object that would, if realized, affect that object's interests. Claims range from decorous collective expressions of support to devastating attacks. The inclusion of claims in the definition rules out inadvertent, indirect, and incremental interactions, however, politically consequential. It rules out, for example, the gradual encroachment of one peasant community on the land of an adjacent peasant community. If, on the other hand, one community makes public, collective demands for some portion of its neighbor's land, the two communities move definitively into the zone of contentious politics (McAdam et al., 2007). Governments figure in all contentious politics, although frequently as third parties rather than initiators or objects of claims. But contention in adjacent arenas regularly affects them as well, for example, when street disorders disrupt the delivery of governmental services. In political contention, most forms of contentions are either conventional or confrontational, more rarely, violent. Conventional and confrontational forms of action are most typical of what Charles Tilly call "the social movement repertoire". Large-scale violence always remains a possibility, however faint. Indeed, contentious politics depending on the claim is always affected by ethnicity and deepest ethnic affiliations. Not all citizens in a country would wish to demonstrate against the government for correction of economic, security or elections malpractices. Members of the ethnic group who's the country's leader comes from may not wish to demonstrate or cause riots against their "son" government. This is due to primordial feeling that "we cannot disrupt our own government" (Tilly, 2008).

9.7. Ethnic Parties and Democratic Stability

Ethnic parties are defined as political parties formed on exclusive particular ethnic outfit (Chol, 2021). They are not mostly based on national ideology but on ethnic card. They exist to champion the interest of their ethnic categories and exclude others and that make such representation central to its strategy of mobilizing voters. Ethnic divisions, according to empirical democratic theory, and common-sense understandings of politics, threaten the survival of democratic institutions (Chandra, 2007). One of the principal mechanisms linking the politicization of ethnic divisions with the destabilization of democracy is the so-called *outbidding effect* (Ibid). According to theories of ethnic outbidding, the politicization of ethnic divisions inevitably gives rise to one or more ethnic parties. The emergence of even a single ethnic party, in turn, "infects" the political system leading to a spiral of extreme bids that destroys competitive politics altogether (Ibid).

We can discern from overleaf, the ethnic-based parties in South Sudan.

9.8. The Economy of Ethnicity, Corruption and Political Market Place

Concept of the Economy of Ethnicity

Scholars of ethnic stratification increasingly research the causes and consequences of employment in ethnic economies. Although debate continues on an ethnic economy's definitive characteristics. In its least restrictive sense, the term refers to economic power and wealth owned by members of an ethnic group (Model, 2009). Until quite recently, efforts to identify the conditions that promote the formation of ethnic economies have dominated the scholarly agenda (Bonacich, 1973). Now, however, researchers are turning to the outcomes associated with jobs in the ethnic economy, a highly controversial undertaking, especially with respect to the experiences of its working class.

Edna Bonacich's influential paper published in 1973 on middleman minorities was the first to examine the definitive characteristics of the ethnic economy in advanced capitalist nations. She stresses the ways ethnic owners mobilize co-ethnic resources to enhance the profitability of small and liquidable enterprises. One of the most important of these resources is the formation of horizontal and/or vertical links with other co-ethnic firms. By limiting competition or by lowering the costs of inputs, these linkages create business advantages in a manner of reminiscent of monopolies. "The result is a tremendous degree of concentration in, and domination of, certain lines of endeavour" as

7	Democratic Change Party-DCP	Hon. Onyoti Adigo Nyikwec	11th April 2016	7
8	South Sudan Democratic Front (SSDF)	Hon. Dr. Martin Elia Lomuro	11th April 2016	8
9	National United Democratic Front-NUDF	Hon. Kornelio Kon Ngu	11th April 2016	9
10	United South Sudan Party-USSP	Hon. Clement Juma Mbugoniwia	11th April 2016	10
11	South Sudan Democratic Alliance-SSDA	Hon. Paskalina Philip Waden	11th April 2016	11
12	Sudan African National Union (SANU)	Hon. Theresa Cirisio Iro	13th June 2016	12
13	United Democratic Salvation Front-UDSF	Eng. Joseph Malual Dong	18th August 2016	13
14	National Democratic Party-NDP	Hon. James Aniceto	23rd September 2016	14

Source: Chol, 2021

Table 4: List of Registered South Sudanese Political Parties

S/no	Name of Party	Party's Chairperson	Date of Registration	Registration Number
1	African National Congress (ANC)	Gen. George Kongor Arop	22nd February 2016	1
2	Sudan People's Liberation Movement-SPLM	H.E. Gen. Salva Kiir Mayardit	22nd February 2016	2
3	United South Sudan African Party-USSAP Ustaz. Joseph Ukel Abango 22nd February 2016 3			
4	United Democratic Salvation Front-Mainstream-UDSF-M	Hon. Francis Ben Ataba	22nd February 2016	4
5	National Liberation Party-NLP	Hon. Nkrumah W. Kelueljang	22nd February 2016	5
6	National Congress Party-NCP	Hon. Agnes Poni Lokudu	23rd February 2016	6

argues by Edna Bonacich (Bonacich, 1973). A second, equally important way that ethnic owners exploit ethnic resources is by hiring co-ethnics paid very low wages in exchange for paternalistic benefits, such as on job training or assistance in eventual self-employment.

A third tier of the economy of ethnicity is ethnic business dominance and control via offering of contracts, jobs and government subsidies to members of an ethnic group. This has been quite prevalent in Africa. It has been done as means of extension of economic and political rule.

Ethnic Corruption

There are various definitions of corruption. Corruption is defined as a form of dishonest or unethical conduct by a person entrusted with a position of authority, often to acquire personal benefit (Mitchel, 2018). Corruption may include many activities including bribery and embezzlement, though it may also involve practices that are legal in many countries. Government, or 'political', corruption occurs when an office-holder or other governmental employee acts in an official capacity for personal gain. However, the most appropriate definition is the one advanced by Vito Tanzi (1998) who defines corruption as the intentional non-compliance with the arm's-length principle aimed at deriving some advantage for oneself or for related individuals from this behaviour (Tanzi, 1998).

Economic theory has developed two basic views of corruption, one that considers corruption to be exogenous and the other endogenous to the political process. Applying either theoretical view, three basic types of corruption can be identified: corruption for the acceleration of processes, administrative corruption, and state capture which is akin to deep state. While in most cases, corruption can be attributed to rent appropriation, self-interested individuals seeking to maximize their own personal welfare as well as complicated, ambiguous, and unenforceable laws are also to blame.

Ethnic corruption is well-captured and summarized in Michela Wrong's masterpiece *"It is Our Turn to Eat"* published in June 2009. A majority of African ethnicities view political power as associated with their communities/ethnicities thus a reigning leader would favour his/her community. By doing so, then corruption ensues, beginning from the leader to the ethnic group. This state of affairs is what Jean-Francois Bayart captured vividly in his ground-breaking work as *"The State of Africa: The Politics of Belly"* published in 2009.

In her seminal work *"South Sudan: Civil War, Predation and The Making of Military Aristocracy"*, Clemence Pinaud summarized SPLM/SPLA corruptions through taxes of the refugees' ratios in Itang-Ethiopia; to the distribution of wives to lieutenants; to putting monies in personal accounts of Dr. John Garang's trusted confidantes and to the building of kinship networks (Pinaud, 2014).

Drawing on Marcel Mauss's analysis of 'gifts', the gifts of bride-wealth and wives illustrate how corruption binds the system of political and class domination. Mauss stresses the point that making return gifts is an absolute obligation in order to retain authority and wealth (Mauss, 2011). In the same vein, the 'gift' made by the commanders to their soldiers constituted ways to retain their authority.

Thus, ethnic corruption in South Sudan has been deepened by the grand corruption in the office of the president. Out of the sixteen individuals accused, ten are from Dinka ethnic group, making total of 63 percent. Out the then individuals acquitted by the Supreme Court, all were from Dinka ethnic group. Drawing from her extensive research, in her book *"The Thieves of State"* Sarah Chayes argues that corruption is a threat to ethnic group, and national and global security (Chayes, 2016). Corruption has no colour or border.

Political Market Place

Corruption has been associated with a daily struggle for primitive accumulation of wealth and power in the political market place (Chol,

2021). Drawing from his much celebrated work *"When Kleptocracy becomes Insolvent: Brute Causes of The Civil War in South Sudan"*, Alex De Waal, argues that members of the South Sudanese political elite, in their desire to acquire wealth as fast as possible, and determination to prevent the northern government from renting the allegiance of southern militia and thereby jeopardizing the SPLM's secessionist project, created a governing system even less regulated and no less brutal than its northern counterpart (De Waal, 2014). Untrammeled greed, combined with the reckless decision to shut down national oil production, meant that by 2013 the South Sudanese government simply could not afford the loyalty payments to keep the system running, and it fell apart. A commander or a provincial leader can lay claim to a stake of state resources (rents) through a mutiny or rebellion. The government then attacks the leader and his constituency to press him to accept a lower price. After a number of people have been killed, raped, and displaced, and their property looted or destroyed, as an exercise in ascertaining the relative bargaining strengths of the two parties, a deal will be reached. In South Sudan, these cycles have become known as "rent-seeking rebellions" (Ibid). Such conflicts follow a material logic but have ethnic manifestations.

Inverting its original intent, the SPLM became a magnet for rent-seekers. However, corruption had permeated the armed struggle from the earliest days and SPLM and SPLA was turned into a marketplace. Peter Adwok Nyaba cited a shocking case of how food rations for conscripts in Ethiopia – which may in fact have been an aid initially destined for refugees were sold and given as *masadaat* (assistance), contributing to deaths by disease and starvation of many hundreds of young recruits (Nyaba, 1997). Over the years, SPLA officers became oriented toward an apparently unending supply of international humanitarian aid, which could be stolen with impunity (De Waal, 2014). Looting of food aid was elevated to military strategy in the 1990s, when the contending factions of the SPLA staged hunger camps to attract humanitarian relief, which was then stolen. SPLA officers also sold natural resources including gold and timber to finance the war effort and themselves, leading some to speak of "blood teak". During the war years SPLA commanders became "military aristocrat", using a raft of coercive, corrupt, and patrimonial measures (Pinaud, 2014). Pinaud's analysis showed how in South Sudan corruption evolved into a political and military marketplace.

9.9. Ethnic Cleavages and Armed Conflict in Congo and Burundi

Ethnic cleavages are defined as differences within ethnic groups that could either enhance peace or trigger armed conflicts across the world. In the case of the Democratic Republic of Congo and Burundi, Ethnic cleavages have promoted violence. I will look at each case, analyse the ethnic cleavage (s) and determine the impact of the conflict and violent.

1. Democratic Republic of Congo (DRC) Conflict
The cause of conflict and violence in DRC is summarized by Jason K. Stearns in his work "Dancing in the Glory of Monsters: The Collapsed of Congo and Great War of Africa" published in 2012. Stearns argued that the civil war was fought by various ethnic groups, particularly, Tutsis and Hutus (Stearns, 2012). The First Congo War began in 1996 as Rwanda grew increasingly concerned that members of Rasemblement Democratique Pour la Rwanda Hutu militias, who were carrying out cross-border raids from Zaire, were planning an invasion of Rwanda. The militias, mostly Hutu, had entrenched themselves in refugee camps in eastern Zaire, where many had fled to escape the Tutsi-dominated Rwandan Patriotic Front (RPF) in the aftermath of the Rwandan Genocide of 1994.

The new Tutsi-dominated RPF government of Rwanda (in power from July 1994) protested this violation of Rwandan territorial integrity and began to give arms to the ethnically Tutsi Banyamulenge of eastern Zaire. The Mobuto government of Zaire vigorously denounced this intervention but possessed neither the military capability to halt it nor the political capital to attract international assistance.

With active support from Uganda, Rwanda, and Angola, the Tutsi forces of Laurent Desire-Kabila moved methodically down the Congo River, encountering only light resistance from the poorly trained, ill-disciplined forces of Mobutu's crumbling regime. The bulk of Kabila's fighters were Tutsis, and many were veterans of various conflicts in the Great Lakes region of Africa. Kabila himself had credibility as a long-time political opponent of Mobutu, and had been a follower of Patrice Lumumba (the first Prime Minister of the Independent Congo), who was executed by a combination of internal and external forces in January 1961, to be replaced by Mobutu in 1965.

The ethnic violence between Hutu and Tutsi aligned forces has been a driving impetus for much of the conflict, with people on both sides fearing their annihilation. The Kinshasa and Hutu aligned forces enjoyed close relations as their interests in expelling the armies and proxy forces of Uganda and Rwanda dovetail.

While the Uganda and Rwanda aligned forces worked closely together to gain territory at the expense of Kinshasa, competition over access to resources created a fissure in their relationship. There were reports that Uganda permitted Kinshasa to send arms to the Hutu FDLR via territory held by Uganda backed rebels as Uganda, Kinshasa and the Hutus are all seeking, in varying degrees, to check the influence of Rwanda and its affiliates. However, the ethnic cleavages of Hutus and Tutsis led to deep division, caused the war and sustained it.

2. Burundi Conflict and Violence

The genesis of Burundian conflict and violence is succinctly captured by Rene Lemarchand in his seminal work "Burundi: Ethnic Conflict and Genocide" published by Woodrow Centre Press in 1996 as an ethnic tweak conflict (Lemarchand, 1996).

The Burundian civil war lasted from 1993 to 2005, and an estimated 300,000 people were killed (Ibid). The conflict ended with a peace process that brought in the 2005 constitution providing guaranteed representation for both Hutu and Tutsi, and parliamentary elections that led to Pierre Nkurunziza, from the Hutu Forces for Defense of Democracy (FDD), becoming President. In Burundi, ethnic differences between Hutu and Tutsi, much as in the case of neighboring Rwanda, existed prior to colonial rule but were solidified by colonial and post-colonial politics. The fight for control of the Burundian state has long been a place where conflict becomes ethnic (Jones, 2015). Approximately 84 percent of Burundians are Hutu, 15 percent are Tutsi, and 1 percent are Twa. Among Burundians, ethnicity is not a taboo subject!

Burundi's history of ethnic violence precedes its civil war (1993-2005), which began after elements of the Tutsi-dominated army assassinated the Hutu president, kicking off ethnic massacres by both groups. One haunting example is the 1972 genocide committed against Hutu elites, schoolboys, army personnel and politicians. Since the outbreak of protests against Pierre Nkurunziza's third term, both the government and opposition have used ethnicized rhetoric. For example, the government and pro-government forces claim that the protests are a purely 'urban' phenomenon, with 'urban' used as an implicit cue indicating Tutsi ethnicity. Increases in ethnically charged speech prompted in November, 2015. US former Secretary of State, John F. Kerry and others called for an immediate cessation of inflammatory dialogue.

More concerning than the rhetoric, however, was the ethnic patterns of violence that emerged to be emerging. There were reports, for example, that security forces targeted protesters in Tutsi minority-heavy districts of Bujumbura in December 2015 (Jones, 2015). These individuals were arrested, tortured and subjected to other forms of violence. Weekend violence resulted in at least 87 deaths, and witness statements and information on victims' ethnicity strongly suggest that many of the victims were disproportionately Tutsi (Ibid).

9.10. Ethnic Politics as Conflict by Other Means, The Case of Kenya

Kenya is a multi-ethnic society and has more than 40 ethnic communities that have lived side by side for a long time. The most dominant ethnic communities in this linguistic and ethnic landscape are the Gikuyu, the Luyha, the Luo, the Kalenjin, the Kamba, and the Kisii. There are however many other smaller ethnic communities in Kenya. Since the onset of colonialism, power in Kenya has been associated with a particular ethnic group. Kenya was initially a protectorate and later a colony of the United Kingdom. From self-rule in 1963 until the death of the first President Mzee Jomo Kenyatta in 1978, political and economic power was increasingly vested in his trusted circle of fellow Kikuyu (Decalo, 1998). During the second presidential regime, political power became concentrated in the hands of Kalenjin élites. In all the different regimes then and after, the ruling group sought to use the resources of the state for the special benefit of its own ethnic community and its allies. It is often suggested that land scarcity and its distribution, which was aggravated by other factors such as a high rate of population growth and environmental degradation, has contributed to the violent ethnic clashes in Kenya.

Since the 1920s, political and economic factors have encouraged the movement of populations within Kenya's national borders, often to zones where they constitute ethnic minorities. The British divided the Kenyan territory along ethnic lines into eight regions with forty-seven counties, creating a different majority in each. Each region was subdivided into county, often according to ethnic groups and subgroups. For example, the Luo are based mainly in Nyanza (though it is also the home to the Kisii, who have their own county); the Luhya, in western region; the Kikuyu, in central region; the Somali, in north-eastern region; and the Mijikenda, in the coastal region. The Rift Valley is dominated by the Kalenjin, but also contains the Maasai, Turkana, Samburu and a number of Kikuyus. The Kamba share eastern region with Embu and Meru, among others. Nairobi is the most cosmopolitan region, with the Kikuyu forming a plurality. Nonetheless, these population movements into ethnically distinct areas did not cause any large-scale violent attacks prior to 1991. Historically, members of Kenya's 40 plus ethnic groups have co-existed, traded and intermarried, often in a symbiotic relationship between pastoralist and agricultural communities (Lonsdale, 1992). Moreover, ethnicity was prior to the mid-twentieth century, a more fluid concept than commonly supposed (Ogot, 1996).

Historical Causes of Ethnic Politics

One of the long-term causes of the clashes in Kenya is attributed to the colonial legacy, which is essentially historical but with ramifications in the post-independence era. It is a historical fact that the indirect rule administered by the British colonialists later turned out to be the 'divide and rule' strategy, which polarized the various ethnic groups in Kenya. This in turn contributed to the subsequent incompatibility of these ethnic groups as actors on in one nation-state called Kenya. It was unfortunate that the early political parties in Kenya that championed the nationalist struggle against colonial establishments were basically distinct ethnic unions. The Kikuyu for instance, formed the Kikuyu Central Association (KCA), the Akamba formed the Ukambani Members Association (UMA), the Luhya formed the Luhya Union (LU), the Luo formed the Young Kavirondo Association (YKA), the Kalenjin formed the Kalenjin Political Alliance (KPA), the coastal tribes formed the Mwambao Union Front (MUF), Taita formed the Taita Hills Association (THA) in that order of ethnic conglomerations (Diamond,

1966). As a result of the foregoing ethnic trends, a situation prevailed in Kenya in which a common political voice was not possible. At the dawn of independence, African leaders ascended to governmental structures which had been intended to preserve the colonial administrative legacy. Indeed, leadership, for example, ruling elites in post-colonial Kenya have often relied heavily on ethnicity to remain in leadership positions or settle a dispute with their perceived enemies.

The land is yet another source of ethnic conflicts in Kenya, both in the long term and in the short term. For a long time in the history of this country, land has remained a thorny economic and political issue. Various scholars like Christopher Leo and Mwangi wa Githumo, have attempted to provide some explanations as to why land has been a major source of ethnic/political conflicts (Wrong, 2009). The land issue has its origin in the colonial history of Kenya, where the colonialists dreamed of making this part of Africa a white man's country. The colonialists established the Kenya protectorate and later on the Kenya colony with the finance that was to be generated from the white settler plantations which covered the high potential areas of the country. History has it that large tracts of agriculturally potential land, for instance, white highlands were alienated by the British colonial administration. As a result of the massive land alienation activities in the early period of colonialism, many of the hitherto cultivating populations were pushed into the 'infertile' native reserves that were not conducive for arable farming. The displaced populations lived as farm laborers, casual workers, tenants as well as squatters. The process of land alienation was also extended to pastoral ethnic groups like the Maasai, Samburu, Nandi, Pokot and other Kalenjin-speaking communities.

Like their agricultural counterparts, the pastoralists were pushed to the less conducive reserves. During the period of nationalism and decolonization, land grievances were central to all ethnic groups that actively participated in the struggle for independence. In fact, the land question is one of the main factors for the Mau Mau rebellion of 1952 to 1956 in Kenya and the subsequent declaration of a state of emergency by the British. After this historic resistance to land alienation by the Africans, the British became very conscious in dealing with the issue of transferring power to the Kenyans at independence. Indeed, the colonialists were afraid that if the land issue was not handled properly, it could degenerate into civil strife as numerous ethnic groups engaged in the scramble to recover their alienated pieces of land.

It is on record that the largest beneficiaries of this land distribution programme were the Kikuyu and their allies, thus the Embu and Meru. By projecting some mythological kinship and taking advantage of neighbourliness, the Kikuyu managed to win the Embu and Meru into some 'land alliance' within the framework of Gikuyu Embu Meru Association (GEMA), which was a bargaining organ for these communities on the sharing of the 'national cake'. The Kikuyu with their allies quickly formed land-buying companies and cooperatives with the blessing of Mzee Jomo Kenyatta. The critics of GEMA have often stated that the membership of these land-buying companies and cooperatives was strictly ethnical-contrary to constitutional and company law provisions against this form of discrimination. Where did they get the money from? The critics further argue that the Kikuyu ethnic group which constituted the membership of these organizations was just as poor as other Kenyan ethnic groups. And yet they managed to buy some of the largest and most expensive tracts of land from white settlers. One possibility is that they raised money from their meagre incomes. But this alone would not certainly have sufficed. The main source was banks and non-bank financial institutions into which President Kenyatta had appointed mostly Kikuyu managers. For instance, the top management of the Kenya Commercial Bank, the National Bank of Kenya and the Industrial and Commercial Development Corporation (ICDC) were registered of managers from one ethnic group. Given this ethnic and political marginalization, other communities from Rift

Valley formed a political union for survival, hence the Kalenjin Maasai Turkana Samburu Association (KAMATUSA).

By 1978 when President Kenyatta died, the Kikuyu had far more than all other ethnic groups put together, bought the bulk of the so-called "white highlands". Besides, they were the main beneficiaries of the government's settlement plan for the landless at no cost or at minimal rates. They thus expanded their land ownership and settlement beyond their traditional home-Central Province into the Rift Valley Province, and a bit into the Coast Province, apart from their widespread networks in urban centres within Kenya. The distribution of land formerly occupied by the white settlers to Kikuyu people mainly, was perceived by other ethnic groups as unfair and there were parliamentary debates that called for equal distribution. Unfortunately, these debates did not address the issue of ethnic imbalance (Eshiwani, 1991), and the subsequent animosity that later on degenerated into the ethnic conflicts between the Kikuyu and the Kalenjins in the Rift Valley.

The issue of unequal distribution of resources is yet another source of potential instability in Kenya. Apart from their easy access to land, the economic success of the Kikuyu region in the first ten years of Kenya's independence was enviable by other ethnic groups. The Kikuyu also enjoyed good modern roads, abundant school and education facilities, expanded health services, piped water, electricity and other forms of infrastructure (Arthur, 1979). More than that GEMA helped its members to acquire land and businesses. They visibly outdistanced other ethnic groups at a pace that posed immediate political risks to their newly acquired positions in the government structures.

In sharp contrast, Nyanza region, the home of the Luo ethnic group suffered severe repression and neglect, more than any other region in Kenya for trying to challenge and question the unjust enrichment of one region on what was a 'national cake'. We give a few illustrations with regard to the ethnic suppressions during the Kenyatta regime. In 1966, Oginga Odinga, the undoubted Luo leader, who had hitherto been the vice president of the nation, and the ruling party, Kenya African National Union (KANU), lost both posts at the famous Limuru Party Conference. The message was clear but milder at this point in time. Odinga responded by forming his political party-the Kenya Peoples Union (KPU). The accusations and counter accusations between Odinga and Kenyatta over KPU were largely emotive and they succeeded in heightening Luo-Kikuyu ethnic tensions and animosities that sometimes degenerated into open confrontations.

The assassinations of Joseph Tom Mboya (an ethnic Luo) for motives never fully ascertained on July 9, 1969, a few months after the mysterious death of Argwings Kodhek, another prominent Luo politician intensified the ethnic animosity between the Luo and the Kikuyu. The banning of KPU in October 1969 and the detention of Odinga and other leaders without trial sent the wrong signals to the Luo ethnic group who could not hide their emotions and anger during the visit of Kenyatta to Kisumu. During this visit, a large crowd of Luo reportedly menaced Kenyatta's security and was fired on by the security guards in what later came to be known as the "Kisumu Massacre". In an explanatory statement, the government accused KPU of being subversive, intentionally stirring up inter-ethnic strife, and accepting foreign money to promote anti-national activities. The prescription in effect returned Kenya to the single party state (Nyukuri, 1997). Following these incidents, Nyanza region, like other non-Kikuyu areas, was virtually written off from national development plans. For instance, the government terminated the construction of the Kenya-Uganda highway (part of a trans-Africa highway system) in 1969 because the road had reached Luo land. The plans to construct the Yala Falls hydro-electric plant were also brought to a halt for spurious reasons.

Other tribes suffered their punishments in the same or varying ways. The same trends of unequal distribution of land, infrastructure and other national resources have been witnessed in the Moi regime, where the Kalenjin ethnic group was "perceived" to have benefitted more than others. However, just like for the Kikuyu, not all Kalenjins have benefited. It is only a clique that surrounds the mantle of power (executive) who seem to have enjoyed in the Moi era (Barasa, 1993).

The mysterious death of Robert Ouko in 1990 strained the relationship between the Luo and Kalenjin ruling elites. This could be considered as one of the long-term causes of the conflicts between the Luo and the Kalenjin in the build up to the 1992 general multi-party elections. I assert that as long as there exist ethnic prejudice and animosity among the diverse Kenyan communities, the search for peace and nation-building will remain elusive.

Another long-term factor of ethnic prejudice and subsequent conflict is attributed to the Africanization of the civil service. Just as there was an immediate need to 'Africanise' the land, the government moved equally fast to give jobs in the civil service and para-government sector to the Africans. Independence had after all been fought for on the popular slogan *"Uhuru na Kazi"* translated as independence will bring jobs. During the colonial period, the African population had worked essentially as plantation laborers or domestic hands for white landowners. It was therefore natural that independence should give them mobility into the higher echelons of the labour market as a realization of self-governance. Understandably, the government came up with a policy, first described as 'Africanization', then 'Kenyanization', and eventually by some unofficial baptism 'Kikuyunization' and 'Kalenjinization'. This terminological mutation succinctly explains how a policy, otherwise well-conceived, deteriorated into the ethnicization of employment in the civil service in Kenya.

Impacts of Ethnic Politics in Kenya
1. Ethnic Violence
Largescale interethnic violence is a new phenomenon in Kenya. The proximate causes of violence are intrinsically related to democratization and the electoral cycle; its roots are to be found in recent times and are

politically instigated, and not primordial. As the move to multipartyism became increasingly probable, senior politicians in many political rallies issued inflammatory statements and utterances, asking for people to go back to their ancestral lands or they be forced out. The advent of the violent ethnic clashes closely followed these rallies (Nyukuri, 1997). As new political parties emerged, a clear enduring pattern of ethno-regional interests appeared. The violence in Kenya appeared to be an ethnicized expression of political conflict. Ethnicity in this case, was the medium of political violence, not its cause. However, the system once in place, became self-perpetuating: it increased the likelihood of future conflict by sharpening ethnic identity and chauvinism, as well as promoting the doctrine that specific regions of the country "belonged" to the groups that "originally" occupied them. This has led to the emergence of terms such as "outsiders," "foreigners," "strangers" or "aliens," and this is regardless of the legal ownership of land and the constitutional right of all Kenyans to live anywhere of their choosing within their country (Ndegwa, 1997).

2. Burden of Electoral Democracy

As explained above, electoral democracy has been a burden, a curse and a regrettable idea for Kenyans. Every year Kenyans carried out elections, particularly, from 1992 to 2022, elections have continued to cause tensions and violence amongst ethnic groups, pitting Kikuyu and Luo or Kikuyu and Kalenjin and others. Kenyan academic and jurist, PLO Lumumba has christened Kenyan elections as an "ethnic census exercise" meaning they are not based on ideology and issues. Thus, electoral democracy has turned out to be electoral ethnic extractions. The multiparty kind of democracy that Kenya has enjoyed so far unfortunately seems to work along ethnic lines although all elections since 1963 have revealed ethnic dimensions. The general elections of 2007 seemed to be a replay of the general elections of 1992, in terms of the ethnic violence that was experienced before and after. This kind of violence in the latest electoral round was large scale and this magnitude had never been witnessed before in all the previous elections. Prior to these elections, the political elites had conducted a lot of campaigns but a closer look at these campaigns revealed that most of them were based on ethnicity and the different ethnic identities that exist in the country. It turned out that the political elites had actually exploited the fact of Kenyan different ethnic identities to forward their political agendas. While the 2022 national elections were ethnically balanced on campaigns and voting, ethnic tensions are still worrying trends in Kenya. While William Ruto won the presidential race through votes and via a Supreme Court ruling, the opposition leader Raila Oding continued to mobilize Kenyans, particularly, his ethnic Luo that William Ruto did not win the August 2022 elections. These mobilizations could make Kenya politically unstable.

3. Kenya, A Deeply Divided Society

With the 2007 post-election violence until today, Kenya has remained a deeply divided country. The 2007 elections led to ethnic violence amongst Kikuyu, Luo and Kalenjin resulting in the deaths of 1,500 persons. The electoral contest between Mwai Kibaki, a Kikuyu and Raila Amolo Odinga, a Luo appeared to be rigged in favour of President Kibaki. A shaky collation government was set up to accommodate Raila and his ODM party. The 2013 elections were also alleged to have been rigged in favour of Uhuru Kenyatta though the Supreme Court ruled in favour of Uhuru. Moreover, the 2017 elections were rigged as the Supreme Court nullified the presidential results, calling for elections with sixty days as per the constitution. Raila Odinga withdrew from the 26th October 2017 elections citing that the Independent Electoral and Boundaries Commission (IEBC) needs reforms to conduct credible, free and transparent elections. Moreover, Raila Odinga disputed August 2022 elections leading to continued demonstrations on Mondays and Thursdays in March 2023. Though President Ruto and Raila have been called to dialogue on issues affecting Kenya. This dialogue is yet to yield the results. It is important to note that Uhuru Muigai Kenyatta, the son of founding father and first President of Kenya, Mzee Jomo Kenyatta and Raila Amolo Odinga, the son of former first Vice President of Kenya, Odinga Oginga have pursued their fathers' bad chemistry which continued to cause tensions and deeply divided Kikuyu and Luo and above all, Kenya today. However, a golden hands-cheque between Raila Odinga and Uhuru Kenyatta normalized the ethnic tensions leading to one empty campaign on Building Bridges Initiative (BBI). It is envisaged that President William Ruto and Raila Odinga may end up in another golden hands-cheque in 2023 to stop Azimio La Umoja violent demonstrations against Kenya Kwanza Government in Kenya.

4. "Nusu Mkate" (Half Loaf of Bread/Coalition) Government

Given all electoral malfeasances, ethnic tensions and conflicts, Kenya went through a mood of *"Nusu Mkate"* (half loaf of bread) governments. We saw this in 2008 after post-election skirmishes where the position of Prime Minister was created to accommodate Raila Odinga and his supporters' given allegations of massive rigging of the polls. However, it appeared that in the August 2022 elections Raila Odinga has not been accommodated in the cabinet-giving Raila Odinga sleepless nights. This mentality of *"Nusu Mkate"* government will continue to haunt Kenya's peace and democracy in the foreseeable future.

9.11. Rwanda Genocide and its Consequences

Origins, Factors and Roots of Genocide

In 1994, Rwanda erupted into one of the most appalling cases of mass murder the world has witnessed since the Second World War. Many of the Hutu majority (about 85 percent of the population) turned on the Tutsi (about 12 percent of the population) and moderate Hutu, killing an estimated total of eight hundred thousand people in three months (Uvin, 1998). Since genocide is the most aberrant of human behaviours, it cries out for explanation. To understand this, a short journey through Rwanda's history is necessary. From 1894 until the end of the First World War, Rwanda, along with Burundi and present-day Tanzania, was part of German East Africa. Belgium claimed it thereafter, becoming the administering authority from 1924 to 1962. During their colonial tenure, the Germans and Belgians ruled Rwanda indirectly through Tutsi monarchs and their chiefs (Melvern, 2009). The colonialists developed the so-called Hamitic hypothesis or myth, which held that the Tutsi and everything humanly superior in Central Africa came from ancient Egypt or Abyssinia. The Europeans regarded Hutu and Twa (about 88 percent of the population) as inferior to Tutsi. Sixty years of such prejudicial fabrications inflated Tutsi egos inordinately and crushed Hutu feelings, which coalesced into an aggressively resentful inferiority complex.

During 1933-34, the Belgians conducted a census and introduced an identity card system that indicated the Tutsi, Hutu, or Twa "ethnicity" of each person. In the identity card "ethnicity" of future generations was determined patrilineally; all persons were designated as having the "ethnicity" of their fathers, regardless of the "ethnicity" of their mothers (Mamdani, 2001). This practice, which was carried on until its abolition by the 1994 post-genocide government, had the unfortunate consequence of firmly attaching a sub-national identity to all Rwandans and thereby rigidly dividing them into categories, which, for many people, carried a negative history of dominance-subordination, superiority inferiority, and exploitation-suffering (Berry, 1999). In their "Hutu Manifesto" of 1957, Hutu leaders referred to the identity card categories as "races," thereby evincing how inflexible these labels had become in their minds. In fact, Hutu and Tutsi spoke the same language and practiced similar religions. They also intermarried.

In November 1959, the pro-Hutu PARMEHUTU party led a revolt that resulted in bloody ethnic clashes and the toppling of Kigeli

Rwabugiri (Uvin, 1998). By 1963, these and other Hutu attacks had resulted in thousands of Tutsi deaths and the flight of about 130,000 Tutsi to the neighbouring countries of Burundi, Zaire by then (now the Democratic Republic of the Congo) and Uganda (Mamdani, 2001). The land and cattle that the fleeing pastoral Tutsi left behind were quickly claimed by land-hungry, horticultural Hutu. As a result of the referendum held in 1961, the Monarch was abolished and national election was held under UN supervision in 1961, Gregoire Kayibanda (author of the "Hutu Manifesto") became Rwanda's President-designate. Rwanda was declared independent on 1st July 1962. Supported by the Tutsi-dominated government in Burundi, Rwandan Tutsi refugees there began launching unsuccessful attacks into Rwanda. These invasions were usually followed by brutal Hutu reprisals against local Tutsi. The Hutu government used a failed 1963 invasion as the pretext to launch a massive wave of repression between December 1963 and January 1964, in which an estimated 10,000 Tutsi were slaughtered (Melvern, 2009). All surviving Tutsi politicians still living in Rwanda were executed (Dalliare, 2003). In July 1973, Major Juvénal Habyarimana, a northern Hutu, overthrew Kayibanda, a southerner, and declared himself President of the Second Republic (Melvern, 2009). In those years, his security forces eliminated former President Kayibanda and many of his high-ranking supporters as part of a plan to eradicate serious Hutu opposition. Habyarimana's kin and regional supporters filled high level positions in the government and security forces. Close relatives of the President and his wife dominated the army, Gendarmerie and especially, the Presidential Guard. Under Habyarimana, Rwanda became a single-party dictatorship. He relegated the Tutsi to the private sector. Regulations prohibited army members from marrying Tutsi. Habyarimana also maintained the "ethnic" identity card and "ethnic" quota systems of the previous regime. By the mid-1980s, the number of Rwandan refugees in neighbouring countries had surpassed one-half million. Thousands more were living in Europe and North America

(Berry, 1999). Habyarimana adamantly refused to allow their return, insisting that Rwanda was already too crowded and had too little land, jobs, and food for them. However, the surrounding countries were also poor and had insufficient resources to accommodate both their own citizens and large refugee populations. Rwandan Tutsi refugees in Uganda, together with some Rwandan Hutu refugees, formed the Rwandan Patriotic Front (RPF) and committed themselves to return to Rwanda. During 1990-93, RPF troops conducted a number of assaults into Rwanda from Uganda in unsuccessful attempts to seize power. The fighting caused the displacement of hundreds of thousands of people. Habyarimana retaliated by heightening internal repression against the Tutsi. From 1990 to 1992, Hutu ultra-nationalists killed an estimated two thousand Tutsi (Melvern, 2009).

Owing to European pressure, especially from France, the Rwandan government allowed political parties and press freedom in the early 1990s. The result was more pro-Hutu, anti-Tutsi extremism. The December 1990 issue of a "Hutu Power" Newspaper vilified the Tutsi as the common enemy (Dallaire, 2009). Despite strong opposition from the growing Hutu power movement, Habyarimana's government signed a series of agreements (the Arusha Accords) with the RPF that called for a power-sharing government with the Tutsi, return of Tutsi refugees to Rwanda, and the integration of Tutsi into the armed forces. The RPF was to constitute 40 percent of the integrated military forces and 50 percent of its officer corps. For Habyarimana, the Accords amounted to a suicide note. Hutu Power leaders cried treason. If the Accords were implemented, many Hutu elitists in the government and the military would lose their privileged positions (Melvern, 2009). A significant number of northern Hutu related to or allied with the powerful lineage of Habyarimana's wife were among those who would be adversely affected. Within days of the signing, Radio Rwanda, RTLM (One Thousand Hills Free Radio), and Radio Milles Collines, a new, private station, began broadcasting anti-Accord and anti-Tutsi diatribes from Kigali. RTLM called for lynching and killing actions against Tutsi whom broadcasters called "cockroaches' and 'snakes".

The Trigger of Genocide

On April 6, 1994, President Juvenal Habyarimana decided to fly back from Dar es Salaam to Gregoire Kayibanda International Airport, now Kigali International Airport in the evening. His jet, a Mystere Falcon 50, was a gift from President Francois Mitterrand which was four years old and spotless (Melvern, 2009). Its maintenance was paid for by France, as were the three crew members, who were former French military officers, a pilot, a chief mechanic and a navigator (Dallaire, 2009). Apparently, President Cyprien Ntaryamira of Burundi asked Habyarimana for a lift home (Melvern, 2009). Ntaryamira was tired and his own propeller-driven plane was slower and less comfortable and above all, his wife was in Kigali. The jet was full and boarded by the two Presidents and the accompanied persons. 'At exactly 8:26 pm, I could see the red lights of the plane as it approached', the air traffic controller recalled. He continued: 'As it passed over Masaka Hill, I saw three missiles, the first went over the aircraft and the third under but the second hit the aircraft and it burst into flames' (Melvern, 2009). The presidential jet was struck by a missile and plunged to earth, killing the president and all aboard. Although the identity of Habyarimana's assassins is not publicly known, it is believed that Habyarimana was killed by Hutu extremists in his own military base (Dallaire, 2009). Within the hour following the crash, and prior to its official announcement over the radio, members of the Interahamwe (Hutu militiamen) had begun to set up roadblocks in Kigali. On April 6th and 9th, the young men checked the identity cards of passers-by, searching for Tutsi, members of opposition parties, and human rights activists. Anyone belonging to these groups was set upon with machetes and iron bars. Radio Milles Collines station, RTLM and Kangura newspapers blamed the RPF and a contingent of UN soldiers for Habyarimana's death and urged revenge against the Tutsi (Mamdani, 2001). The Presidential Guard began killing Tutsi civilians in Ramera, a section of Kigali near the airport. Extremists in the President's entourage had made up lists of Hutu political opponents, mostly democrats, for the first wave of murders.

The extremists exhorted the Interahamwe and ordinary Hutu to kill Tutsi and *"eat their cows"* (Uvin, 1998). This phrase had both symbolic and practical significance. Symbolic, because historically Tutsi supremacy had been built on cattle ownership. Practical, because it also meant looting Tutsi homes, farms, offices, businesses, churches, and so on. The theft was one of the main rationales used to bribe people into betraying and killing their neighbours. RPF troops from the north began fighting their way south in early April in an attempt to stop the slaughter. By July 18, the RPF had reached the Zaire (DRC) border. Having defeated the Hutu militias that opposed them, the RPF unilaterally declared a cease-fire. Within a period of only three months (100 days) over seven hundred and fifty thousand Tutsi and between ten thousand and forty thousand Hutu, amounting to around eight hundred thousand or 11 percent of the total population, had been killed (Melvern, 2009). About two million people were displayed within Rwanda, while similar number of Hutu fled from Rwanda into Tanzania, Burundi, and Zaire (Uvin, 1998). The RPF and moderate Hutu political parties formed a new government on July 18, 1994, but the country was in chaos. The government pledged to implement the Arusha Accords. The government publicly committed itself to building a multiparty democracy and to discontinuing the ethnic classification system utilized by the previous regime.

The Role of Colonialist/Western Powers in Genocide
Mahamood Mamdani in his ground-breaking work *"When Victims Become Killers: Colonialism, Nativism, and the Genocide in Rwanda."* argued that the Rwandan genocide needs to be thought of within the logic of

colonialism (Mamdani, 2001). The horror of colonialism led to two types of genocidal impulses. The first was the genocide of the native by the settler; the second was the native impulse to eliminate the settler. Following Franz Fanon, Mamdani says the second seemed more like the affirmation of the native's humanity than the brutal extinction of life. The Tutsi, a group with a privileged relationship to power before colonialism, was constructed as a privileged alien settler presence, first by the Hutu revolution of 1959, and then by Hutu Power propaganda after 1990. During the colonial period and thereafter, "Hutu" was made into a native identity and "Tutsi" a settler one. In its motivation and construction, Mamdani further argued, the Rwandan genocide needs to be understood as a natives' genocide. It was a genocide by those who saw themselves as sons and daughters of the soil, and their mission was one of clearing the soil of a threatening alien presence. It was not an ethnic, but a "racial" cleansing. For the Hutu who killed, the Tutsi were colonial settlers, not a neighbour. Most scholars on the subject traced Hutu-Tutsi distinction to the Belgians' use of the ten-cow rule for the 1933-34 census and the identity cards. Supposedly, any male who owned 10 cows was classified as a Tutsi; those with fewer than 10 cows were classified as Hutu. No explanation for Twa is usually given. Relying on a doctoral dissertation by Tharcisse Gatwa, (2000), Mamdani writes that the Belgians actually used three major sources of information for their census classification: "oral information provided by the church, physical measurements, and ownership of large herds of cows" (Gatwa, 2000). The fact is," writes Mamdani, "that the Belgian power did not arbitrarily cook up the Hutu/Tutsi distinction." What it did was to take an existing socio-political distinction and radicalized it (Ibid). The origin of the violence in Rwanda is connected to how Hutu and Tutsi were constructed as political identities by the colonial state, Hutu as indigenous and Tutsi as alien.

Indeed, as the genocide unfolded, France supported Hutus while Belgium supported Tutsi. The USA and UK did not help but ended up lobbying the UNSC in the withdrawal of 25,000 UNAMIR after ten Belgians soldiers were killed. The UN did not heed the advice of Canadian Commander of UNAMIR, Lieutenant General Romeo Alain Dallaire who called for the UN action before widespread genocide but the UN was silent. He asked for more troops to stop violence but UN refused. In his seminal book *"Shaking Hands with the Devil: The Failure of Humanity in Rwanda, (2003)"* Lt. Gen. Romeo attributed genocide to the failure of Western powers to act as told. The UN then admitted its failure and UNSC accepted its responsibility for not preventing genocide. In her thought-provoking book *"A People Betrayed: The Role of The West in Rwanda's Genocide"*, Linda Melvern examined the failure of UN member governments to comply with the 1948 Genocide Convention and the shock waves Rwanda caused around the world. Instead, in November 1994, the United Nations Security Council (UNSC) passed a resolution that created the International Criminal Tribunal for Rwanda (ICTR) (Brehm, et al., 2014). The mandate of this ad-hoc tribunal was to try the Rwandans deemed most responsible for the genocide. The ICTR held its first trial in Arusha, Tanzania, in 1997 and handed down the world's first conviction by an international court for the crime of genocide 1 year later. As of 2021, the tribunal has completed 90 cases.

Consequences of the Genocide

In the aftermath of the genocide in Rwanda, the RPF overthrew Hutu government in July 1994. Half a million women and girls were tortured, raped and abused acquiring sexual transmitted diseases, especially HIV / AIDS (Berry, 1999). Over two hundred and fifty thousand children have been orphaned by these diseases(Melvern, 2009). Many people got into trauma and have mental problems (Uvin, 1998). Property, homes, schools, roads and churches were destroyed. Poverty expanded (Mamdani, 2001). Many criminals were jailed and Gacaca court system was introduced in 2001. Gacaca in Kinyarwanda refers to *"grass"*. Thus, Gacaca court refers to *'justice on the grass"*. In more than nine thousand clans throughout Rwanda, panels of elected lay judges known as Inyangamugayo *("those who detest dishonesty" in Kinyarwanda)* presided over genocide trials in the same cities, towns, and villages where the crimes were committed (Rettig, 2008). More than 250,000 male and female judges were elected, and in April 2002, the elected judges underwent training. Finally, on June 18, 2002, the first pilot phase of the Gacaca began.

What is more, the Government of Rwanda and international organizations played a great role in the post-reconstruction and reconciliation of the country. In March 2003, Paul Kagame won the first national election. President Kagame reshaped the identity of Rwandans, he abolished through the constitution, the ethnic identities of Hutu and Tutsi. The population was to be referred to as Rwandans and Kinyarwanda became the national language. Thus, all three ethnic groups, Hutu, Tutsi and Twa proudly called themselves Rwandans. Moreover, Kagame introduced a community service day called 'Umuganda" referring to *"our pride"* in Kinyarwanda. This occurs on the last Saturday of every month when all Rwandans including the President volunteer to clean the environment. It is a day meant to cement national unity and identity. Besides, as part of deepening reconciliation, national unity and development, the Government of Rwanda introduced in November 2003, an annual national dialogue referred to as *"Umushyikirano"* in Kinyarwanda. The President visits each province annually and engages directly with the common citizens in town halls, meeting grounds or stadiums.

9.12. Accommodation of Deep Ethnic Differences and National Identities

Ethnic identity is salient cleavage that is highly mobilized in political conflicts in the developing world. From Asia to Caribbean to the Middle East and to Africa, ethnic cards are played in achieving political goals (Chol, 2014). Accommodating deep ethnic differences and national identities goes back to Arend Lijphart's "theory of consociationalism" exhaustively discussed hi his masterpiece- "The Politics of Accommodation". Yet, Lipjhart's *Theory of Consociationalism* which would have served as the treatment of the deeply divided society was misunderstood and wrongly applied by many Republics (Lijphart, 2009). Lijphart's thinking was not a political accommodation of the individuals but the representation of all cross-cutting cleavages of the societies such as ethnic groups, political parties, elites and minorities' autonomies in the governance etc. Lijphart institutional design model offers accommodation with legal redress and social justice and thus the new Republics such as South Sudan, DRC and Burundi concentrated on the mere political and military accommodation of individuals without addressing crimes committed by the accommodated individuals in the first place. This led to impunity; rebellions and re-rebellions of the individuals tweaked on rewards and amnesties. Thus, this compromised social justice.

Accommodating deep identity differences begin with what unites the people in that country and what values do communities in that polity cherish. From Nigeria, Ethiopia, Somalia, South Sudan, Sudan, Burundi, DRC, Iraq, Spain, Lebanon, Yemen etc, identity conflict has ensued in a variety of ways. Some have graduated from localized conflicts to insurgencies and then to outright civil wars, some have stuck in permanent rebellions. Although Lijphart's consociational theory is a treatment to the deeply divided identities, *co-identities theory* (author's term) is a solution to sensitive national identities.

Moreover, many experts uncritically promote federalism in its various forms as a panacea for multicultural societies with deep community cleavages, notably those coming out of ethnic wars (Watts & Chattopadhyay, 2008). According to some recent scholars' federal arrangements offer the best option for governance designed to reflect diversity and consociation, in terms of political recognition and representation. However, in multi-ethnic/multi-cultural societies, the quality of governance and accommodating diversity depends heavily on the type of democracy within which they function. For instance, either majoritarian or consensual (Fleiner, 2008). It is interesting to note that globally, the power-sharing constitutions combining proportional representation and federalism are relatively few (seventeen out of one hundred and ninety-six States (Watts and Chattopadhyay, 2008). Indeed, empirical evidence suggests that proportional representation-based electoral systems, and not federalism or other types of power-sharing arrangements, are not adequate for democratic inclusion and participation. The implications for policymakers are clear: investing in basic human development is probably a more reliable route to achieve stable democratic governance than mere constitutional design (Norris, 2005). "We the people" should be translated into reality and practice as stipulated in many countries' constitutions.

CHAPTER TEN

10.1. Ideologies from Different Platforms of the World

10.2. What is an Ideology?

Ideology is a term, which has caused heated debate and argument in political science. Karl Mannthiem (1946) defined it as "a pattern of beliefs that justifies a social order and which explains to man his historical and social setting" (Mannthiem, 1946). A more recent definition is that "it a set of closely related beliefs or ideas, or even attitudes, characteristic of a group or community which is both 'descriptive and persuasive" (Plamenatz, 1970). Ideology also refers to a systematized and interconnected set of ideas about the organization of the economic, political and socio-cultural aspects of society in entirety. Any ideology therefore prescribes the best kind of political system and economic systems and the best kind of socio-cultural structure that are necessary to promote the happiness and welfare of citizens.

The word ideology comes from late-eighteenth century French thinker, Count Antoine Destutt de Tracy (1754-1836), to designate the science or study of ideas that he had devised and which he was anxious to popularize. However, it was Napoleon first used the concept of ideology as a critical term to disparage false systems of ideas held by his political opponents. In this respect, he was followed by Karl Marx, who used it to refer to the notions of his German rivals, which prevented them from seeing as he did the logically compelling nature of the real truths of politics.

Countries can therefore be distinguished on the basis of the kind of ideology that is dominance within their boundaries that will in turn determine the nature of political systems. Although many ideologies exist all over the world, only a few have had a fundamental influence on the political systems of given States. There are four ideologies as follows:

1. Liberalism and capitalism
2. Socialism and Fascism
3. Marxism
4. Nationalism

Ideologies influence the kind of constitution, governmental, structures, laws and rules that govern the management of public affairs.

10.3. Ideology in the First World Group of States

Most countries in the 1ˢᵗ world have been influenced by the liberal democratic ideology, which has further influenced their politics and economic systems. For example, most of them practice comparative party politics in which the rule of law is practiced and respect for human rights and freedoms are emphasized. Moreover, such states practice capitalist mode of production, which includes freedom of enterprise whereby individuals and groups of people can own property privately. Examples of countries that are influenced by liberal ideology are found in Western Europe and North America as well as Australia and New Zealand. However, liberal democracy has increasingly begun to influence political system in some countries outside of the first world group.

10.4. Ideology in the Second World Group of States

In the second world group of states, the ideology that has been dominant is Marxism, which advocates for a communist or socialist mode of production, which in the interim time emphasizes single-party system, as well as public ownership of the means of production. Moreover, the government rigidly controls people's economic, social, cultural and political aspects of life. Examples include the former Soviet Union, former Yugoslavia, China, North Korea, Cuba and Poland. However, following the collapse of the Soviet Union in 1991, the influence of Marxist ideology in the political systems is increasingly fading away and most of these political systems are increasingly coming under the influence of liberalism.

10.5. Ideology in the Third World Group of States

Since independence, third-world states have been influenced by various ideologies while some have been influenced by liberalism. Others have been influenced by Marxist ideas, for example, those that practice socialism, which was spread in various regions in the world including Africa, Asia and Latin America. Some countries in the third world have tried to come up with their own brand of ideology. For instance, socialism in Africa was adopted by countries such as Tanzania, Senegal and even Kenya. African Socialism (Ujamaa) was a blend of the scientific socialism of Eastern Europe and traditional African ways of life, which emphasize communal living.

Apart from African Socialism, some countries in Africa and the third world in general have been influenced by fascist principles and this is particularly so in the case of military governments and single-party dictatorships which adopted certain fascist methods, such as the use of terror, abuse of human rights and denial of fundamental freedoms and basic human equality.

Finally, third-world states have also made extensive use of nationalism as a convenient tool to mobilize support and overcome opposition by stressing internal or external threats to national unity. Thus, governments have always emphasized patriotism and national unity and these are key aspects of nationalism as an ideology.

CHAPTER ELEVEN

11.1. Comparative Political Institutions of Governments

11.2. What are Political Institutions?

Political institutions refer to both the formal organs as well as informal structures, which bear upon deliberation and decision-making, the former including the government, the parliament, the courts, and the administrative staff and the latter including constituencies and regions (Chol, 2021). Institutions refer to rules, procedures, systems, policies, regulations and laws that work in constraint in a polity (Common, 2002).

Political institutions are social instrumentalities for the attainment of community goals. While informal institutions exert great influence on decision-making through such input functions as political socialization, communication, interest-articulation and interest aggregations, they also exert their influences through the formal organs and structures that the output functions. These decisions are officially formulated, expressed and realized or emphasis will be on the formal structures of political institutions.

The familiar structures within political systems include: interest groups, political parties, legislatures, executives, bureaucracies and courts. Countries have these political institutions but they are not only organized differently, they function very differently indeed. Thus, institution by institution comparisons must spell out functions in detail before it can bring us toward understanding the important similarities and differences in the politics of these countries. It is when we separate structure or institution from function and trace these activities through the inputs, the conversion process and outputs of the political system that we can arrive at a judgment of the significance of the various political institutions. Bingham Powell (1988) assert that only when we start to ask questions about the process and performance we can attach meaning to structural characteristics (Powell, 1988). It is when we come to the point that we can say specific institutions perform specific functions with specific consequences does our comparative analysis begin to make some sense.

11.3. Why Study Political Institutions?

In the political context, institutions are primarily organizations. It is necessary to state that institutions and ideologies operate political systems. However, there are some institutions and structures that play leading roles in the formulation of public policy. According to John Loewestern (1965), institutions are the apparatus through which the power process functions in a society organized as a state (Loewestern, 1965). The dynamics of politics, that is, decision-making is constituted by the interplay between social organs.

In addition, institutional comparison focuses on the way legal authority is distributed among these institutions in accordance with constitutional principles and other statutory provisions. What are the powers of the President of the United States vis-à-vis the Congress? What is the legal authority of the British House of Commons and House of Lords? What are the express legal powers of the Presidents of France, Germany, Russia, Mexico and South Africa? And above all, why do States distribute legal authority the way they do? In most countries the legal competence of the leading governmental institutions is spelled out in their constitution. The legislatures, the world over, irrespective of whether they are operating in the developed democracies or the industrialized states or found in the developing countries are generally perceived to have declined in terms of their ability to efficiently and realistically perform the roles with which they are often associated with in the modern states.

However, while most scholars believe that the legislatures have declined in performance, there are some scholars who still stick to the position that the realities of the complex socio-economic and political environment are clearly visible. Whereas the legislatures don't only support transformational roles, they also have great involvement of different assemblies in the policy-making activities of the different States of the world (Blondel, 1969).

This development is, indeed, a contradiction largely because the representative assembly is believed to symbolize the peoples' sovereignty. In fact, Margaret Davies (1996) noted that democracy loses its essence and becomes meaningless without the existence of a viable, functional and potent legislature (Davies, 1969). Scholars like Jean Blondel (1969) are of the view that most other scholars are having a wrong notion of what legislatures should do and what they actually do (Blondel, 1969). To Blondel, this wrong notion arises from the fact that there is a huge expression from the public that the legislatures should be at the vanguard of public policy making. By this, they are bereft of the knowledge of the constraint that the operating environment, characterized by the high level of complexity and technicality is imposed on the legislatures. Consequently, rather than restricting themselves to law-making, modern assemblies are often deeply involved in scrutiny and oversight of the activities of the administration. The degrees to which the assemblies are involved in the affairs of their respective states also vary significantly. A brief explanation of a few cases may suffice. In doing this, it is important to examine both the parliamentary and presidential systems of government.

11.4. Parliamentary System of Government

A parliamentary system is a system of government wherein the ministers of the executive branch are drawn from the legislature, and are accountable to that body, such that the executive and legislative branches are intertwined. In such a system, the head of government is both *de facto* chief executive and chief legislator. Parliamentary systems are characterized by no clear-cut separation of powers between the executive and legislative branches, leading to a different set of checks and balances compared to those found in presidential systems. Parliamentary systems usually have a clear differentiation between the head of government and the head of state, with the head of government being the prime minister or premier, and the head of state often being a figurehead, often either a president (elected either popularly or by the parliament) or a hereditary monarch (often in a constitutional monarchy). A parliamentary system may consist of two styles of chambers of parliament, one with two chambers (or houses): an elected lower house, and an upper house or senate which may be appointed or elected by a different mechanism from the lower house. This style of two houses is called bicameral system. Legislatures with only one house are known as unicameral system.

The parliamentary system does not mean that different parties in coalition with each other rule a country. Such multiparty arrangements are usually the product of an electoral system known as proportional representation. Many parliamentary countries, especially those that use "first past the post" voting, have governments composed of one party. However, parliamentary systems in continental Europe do use proportional representation, and tend to produce election results in which no single party has a majority of seats. Proportional representation in a non-parliamentary system doesn't have this result (Arguelles, 2009). Parliamentarianism may also be for governance in local governments. An example is the city of Oslo, which has an executive council as a part of the parliamentary system. The council manager system of municipal government used in some U.S. cities bears many similarities to a parliamentary system. Arend Lijphart (2009) divides parliamentary democracies into two different systems: the Westminster and consensus systems (Lijphart, 2009).

1. The West Minister Model

The Westminster Palace in London, United Kingdom originates from the British Houses of Parliament. Today, the Westminster system is found in many Commonwealths of Nations countries, although they are neither universal within nor exclusive to Commonwealth countries. These parliaments tend to have a more adversarial style of debate and the plenary session of parliament is relatively more important than committees. Some parliaments in this model are elected using a plurality voting system (first past the post), such as the United Kingdom, Canada, and India, while others use proportional representation, such as Ireland and New Zealand. The Australian House of Representatives is elected using instant-runoff voting while the Senate is elected using proportional representation through single transferable vote. Even when proportional representation systems are used, the voting systems tend to allow the voter to vote for a named candidate rather than a party list. This model does allow for a greater separation of powers than the Western European model, since the governing party will often not have a majority in the upper house. However, parliamentary systems still feature a lesser separation of powers than is found in democratic presidential systems. Government in a parliamentary system of the Westminster model is based on the fact that those who constitute the cabinet are drawn from the legislature. Indeed, the chief executive, that is, the head of cabinet, who is the prime minister, is not elected on the strength of popular votes of the public. The prime minister is chosen on the grounds that he is the leader of the party with majority seats in parliament.

What this translates into is that members of the cabinet are drawn from the assembly and also retain their seats as legislators while serving as ministers. This underlines the doctrine of fusion of power commonly associated with the parliamentary system. Largely because members of the cabinet are drawn from and remain members of the legislature, the continual support of the assembly is needed for the government to continue in office (Landman, 2008). The government will cease to exist if it receives a "negative vote", that is, when a vote of no confidence is passed on the government, the government is forced to resign. But the government may dissolve the assembly in turn. However, because of the enormous cost to be paid, particularly by the majority party in parliament, if dissolution takes place, it is a dormant instrument that the house does not apply.

The legislature in the parliamentary system appears much weaker than the legislature in the presidential democracy. This is so because, the survival of the cabinet and government depends on the support of the assembly, hence high party discipline ensures that legislatures elected on the platform of the ruling party exercise less independence during voting on issues in the house. Members of the ruling party in a parliamentary democracy are subordinated to high party control, such as is not common or seen in the presidential arrangement. The laws passed by the entire parliament cannot be reversed or set aside by any Court in the land. This is why it is said that the Westminster parliament is the most powerful in terms of lawmaking. By this, parliamentary legislation is not subject to judiciary review. This contrasts with the practice in most presidential democracies where judicial review is a critical component of the constitutional framework.

The only seeming check on parliamentary power is the power of veto of the King, which is rarely applied. On the other hand, the House of Lords may exercise its power of suspense veto, but such veto is vacated after six months. Thus, the Commons can have its suspended laws passed after the suspense veto lapses. This contrast with the presidential system where the concurrence of the two chambers is required before any bills becomes law. If any of the houses decide not to consider a bill already passed by the other, the bill dies. The British parliament is primarily established on dual institutions. The first being the two-chamber legislature while the second is the cabinet. According to Paul Appadorai (1968), "the cabinet is real, as distinguished, from the nominal executive in Britain" (Appadorai, 1968). What this suggests is that those members drawn from the legislature constitute the real cabinet while the queen or the King, who by inheritance occupies the executive office, is the nominal. Indeed, the power of the executive is believed to be exercised by the cabinet on behalf of the crown. This perhaps explains why the cabinet is taken to be a body of royal advisers chosen by the prime minister in the name of the crown with the tacit approval of the House of Commons. It is important to point out that for King in Parliament, the House of Lords and the House of Commons, constitutes the law-making body in Britain unlike the American presidential model, the parliamentary model is a system where the party that receives or wins the highest seats in parliament forms government. However, in situation where no party receives the majority votes required to form government, coalition of parties will be required to form a government. However, when a coalition is formed by parties with incongruent ideologies and interests, this may result to the frequent dissolution of the government. The system in such an operational environment will become unstable. No case justifies this better than the French fourth republic when on average a government stayed in office for six months before dissolution results from the collapsed coalition. Examples of countries with pure parliamentary system where there exists mutual dependence between executive and legislature include the United Kingdom, the Netherlands, Belgium, Germany, Norway, Sweden, Italy , Iceland and Denmark (Landman, 2008). In these countries, the executive depends on the confidence of the majority (or coalition) in the legislature; the executive can dissolve the legislature (usually in conjunction with the head of state) and lastly no separate elections are needed for each executive and legislature, In the UK, the court is to some extent not too separate from the legislature and the cabinet. This is largely because members of the legislature are chosen to form a cabinet. Yet, every member of cabinet is an automatic member of the Privy Council (Appadorai, 1968). However, not all members of the Privy Council are members of cabinet. This is so because former cabinet members remain members of Privy Council for life. The Privy Council is an appellate court and is the highest court in Britain.

2. The Consensus System

Some Western European parliamentary models (e.g., Spain and Germany) tend to have a more consensual debating system and have semi-cyclical debating chambers. Consensus systems are identified by proportional representation, where there is more of a tendency to use party list systems than the Westminster model legislatures. The committees of these Parliaments tend to be more important than the plenary chamber. This model is sometimes called the West German Model since the earliest exemplar in its final form was in the Bundestag of West Germany (which became the Bundestag of Germany upon the absorption of the Germany Democratic Republic by the Federal Republic of Germany). Switzerland is considered one of the purest examples of a consensus system. There also exists a hybrid model, the semi-presidential system, drawing on both presidential systems and parliamentary systems. For example, the French Fifth Republic. Much of Eastern Europe has adopted this model since the early 1990s.

Implementations of the parliamentary system can also differ on whether the government needs the explicit approval of the parliament to form, rather than just the absence of its disapproval, and under what conditions (if any) the government has the right to dissolve the parliament, like Jamaica and many others. Most of the developing countries inherited the parliamentary arrangement bequeath to them at independence by their formal colonial administrations. But the parliamentary arrangement was largely assaulted and dismantled by the Africans who took over political power at independence. The system of parliamentary democracy adopted by the seventeen former British African countries with the exception of Zambia, Botswana and Zimbabwe Nwabueze (2004) describes the Westminster export model. This model was a by-product of the reform introduced to make the system reflects local realities of the respective states. Thus, as opposed to the typical Westminster or parliamentary tradition of Britain, the inherited parliamentary system in the African States is characterized by:

- The justifiability of relations between organs of the executive and the judicial review of the constitutionality of actions of government, particularly legislative acts;

- The separation of executive and judicial power (as distinct from their personnel) from legislative power. The Constitution is supreme;

- A plural executive but the two executives are politicians unlike in Britain where one is monarch. The system is of plural executive, because the ministers are equal in powers, with the prime ministers as mere primus inter pares. But the prime minister gains pre-eminence by the fact that he forms government and presides over the cabinet;

- The power to make legislation jointly vested in both the legislature and the head of state; and

- The prime minister and other ministers are members of the legislative assembly. The prime minister is the leader of the majority party (Nwabueze, 2004).

However, the parliamentary arrangement inherited by these states collapsed shortly after political independence. The collapse of the parliamentary democracy due to one form of authoritarian party government or transformation to a presidential model was explained away by Adedeji Adebayo (1986) as a mere consequence of the unsuitability of the parliamentary model to a complex, heterogeneous and divided societies as those upon which the system was imposed in Africa (Adebayo, 1986). The argument then was that the imposition of a dual executive was alien to African tradition where only one person was always recognized as the paramount ruler. Thus, a power tussle or contest between two clashing personalities was alien to Africa. This explains the transformation from the parliamentary model to one form of presidentialism. The survival of the parliamentary system in most countries of Europe may therefore be attributed to the history of an age-long practice in those countries.

Advantages of the Parliamentary System

One of the commonly attributed advantages of parliamentary systems is that it's faster and easier to pass legislation. This is because the executive branch is dependent upon the direct or indirect support of the legislative branch and often includes members of the legislature. Thus, this would amount to the executive (as the majority party or coalition of parties in the legislature) possessing more votes in order to pass legislation. In a presidential system, the executive is often chosen independently from the legislature. If the executive and legislature in such a system include members entirely or predominantly from different political parties, then stalemate can occur. Former US President Bill Clinton often faced problems in this regard, since the Republicans used to control Congress for much of his tenure. Accordingly, the executive within a presidential system might not be able to properly implement his or her platform/manifesto. Evidently, an executive in any system (be it parliamentary, presidential or semi-presidential) is chiefly voted into office on the basis of his or her party's platform/manifesto. It could be said then that the will of the people is more easily instituted within a parliamentary system.

In addition to quicker legislative action, Parliamentarianism has attractive features for nations that are ethnically, racially, or ideologically divided. In a unipersonal presidential system, all executive power is concentrated on the president. In a parliamentary system, with a collegial executive, power is more divided. In the 1989 Lebanese Taif Agreement, in order to give Muslims greater political power, Lebanon moved from a semi-presidential system with a strong president to a system more structurally similar to a classical parliamentarianism. Iraq similarly disdained a presidential system out of fears that such a system would be tantamount to Shiite domination; Afghanistan's minorities refuse to go along with a presidency as strong as the Pashtuns desired. Some scholars have also argued that power is more evenly spread out in the power structure of parliamentarianism. To this school of thought, the premier seldom tends to have as high importance as a ruling president, and there tends to be a higher focus on voting for a party and its political ideas than voting for an actual person. For instance, Walter Bagehot (2010) praised parliamentarianism for producing serious debates, for allowing the change in power without an election, and for allowing elections at any time (Bagehot, 2010). Bagehot considered the four-year election rule of the United States to be unnatural (Ibid).

There is also a body of scholarship, associated with Juan Linz, Fred Riggs, Bruce Ackerman, and Robert Dahl that claims that parliamentarianism is less prone to authoritarian collapse. These scholars point out that since the Second World War two-thirds of Third World countries establishing parliamentary governments successfully made the transition to democracy. By contrast, they argue, no Third World presidential system successfully made the transition to democracy without experiencing coups and other constitutional breakdowns. As Bruce Ackerman (2013) says of the thirty countries to have experimented with American checks and balances and thus all of them, without exception, have succumbed to the nightmare (of breakdown) one time or another, often repeatedly (Ackerman, 2013).

Disadvantages of Parliamentary System

One main criticism of many parliamentary systems is that the head of government is in almost all cases not directly elected. In a presidential system, the president is usually chosen directly by the electorate, or by a set of electors directly chosen by the people, separate from the legislature. However, in a parliamentary system the Prime Minister is elected by the legislature, often under the strong influence of the party leadership. Thus, a party's candidate for the head of government is usually known before the election, possibly making the election as much about the person as the party behind him or her. Another major criticism of the parliamentary system lies precisely in its purported advantage: that there is no truly independent body to oppose and veto legislation passed by the parliament, and therefore no substantial check on legislative power. Conversely, because of the lack of inherent separation of powers, some believe that a parliamentary system can place too much power in the executive entity, leading to the feeling that the legislature or judiciary has little scope to administer checks or balances on the executive.

However, parliamentary systems may be bicameral, with an upper house designed to check the power of the lower (from which the executive comes). Although it is possible to have a powerful prime minister, as Britain has, or even a dominant party system, as Japan has, parliamentary systems are also sometimes unstable. Critics point to Israel, Italy, Canada, the French Fourth Republic, and Weimar Germany as examples of parliamentary systems where unstable coalitions, demanding minority parties, votes of no confidence, and threats of such votes, make or have made effective governance impossible. Defenders of parliamentarianism say that parliamentary instability is the result of proportional representation, political culture, and highly polarized electorates. Former Prime Minister Ayad Allawi criticized the parliamentary system of Iraq, saying that because of party-based voting the vast majority of the electorate based their choices on sectarian and ethnic affiliations, not on genuine political platforms.

Also, for allowing an election to take place at any time, without a definite election calendar, it has been pointed out that the Parliamentary system can indeed be abused. In some systems, such as in UK, a ruling party can schedule elections when it feels that it is likely to do well, and so avoid elections at times of unpopularity. Thus, by careful timing of elections, in a parliamentary system a party can extend its rule for longer than is feasible in a functioning presidential system. This problem can be alleviated somewhat by setting fixed dates for parliamentary elections, as is the case in several of Australia's state parliaments. In other systems, such as the Dutch and the Belgian, the ruling party or coalition has some flexibility in determining the election date. Also, critics of parliamentary systems point out that people with significant popular support in the community are prevented from becoming Prime Minister if they cannot get elected to parliament since there is no option to run for Prime Minister like one can run for president under a presidential system. Additionally, prime ministers may lose their positions solely because they lose their seats in Parliament, even though they may still be popular nationally. However, proponents of the Parliamentary system have argued that as members of parliament, prime ministers are elected firstly to represent their electoral constituents and if they lose their support then consequently, they are no longer entitled to be prime minister.

11.5. Presidential System of Government

A presidential system is a system of government where an executive branch exists and presides (hence the name) separately from the legislature, to which it is not accountable and which cannot, in normal circumstances, dismiss it. It owes its origins to the medieval monarchies of France, England and Scotland in which executive authority was vested in the Crown, not in meetings of the estates of the realm (i.e., Parliament): the Estates-General of France, the Parliament of England or the Estates of Scotland. The concept of separate spheres of influence of the executive and legislature was emulated in the Constitution of the United States, with the creation of the office of the President of the United States. In England and Scotland (since 1707 as the Kingdom of Great Britain, and since 1801 as the United Kingdom) the power of a separate executive waned to a ceremonial role and a new executive, answerable to parliament, evolved while the power of the United States separated executive increased. This has given rise to criticism of the United States presidency as an "imperial presidency" though some analysts dispute the existence of an absolute separation, referring to the concept of "separate Institutions sharing power". Although not exclusive to republics, and applied in the case of semi-constitutional monarchies where a monarch exercises power (both as head of state and chief of the executive branch of government) alongside a legislature, the term is often associated with republican systems in the Americas. The defining characteristic of a Republican presidential system is how the executive is elected, but nearly all presidential systems share the following features:

1. The president has a fixed term of office. Elections are held at scheduled times and cannot be triggered by a vote of no confidence or other such parliamentary procedures. In some countries, there is an exception to this rule, which provides for the removal of a president in the event that he/she is found to have broken a law.

2. The executive branch is unipersonal. Members of the cabinet serve at the pleasure of the president and must carry out the policies of the executive and legislative branches. However, presidential systems frequently require legislative approval of presidential nominations to the cabinet as well as various governmental posts such as judges. A president generally has the power to direct members of the cabinet, military or any officer or employee of the executive branch, but generally has no power to dismiss or give orders to judges.

3. The power to pardon or commute sentences of convicted criminals is often in the hands of the heads of state in governments that separate their legislative and executive branches of government.

11.6. The Office of the President

We must note that countries that feature a presidential system of government are not the exclusive users of the title of President or the republican form of government. For example, a dictator, who may or may not have been popularly or legitimately elected maybe and often is called a President. Likewise, many parliamentary democracies are republics and have Presidents, but this position is largely ceremonial; notable examples include Germany, India, Ireland and Israel. Some national Presidents are "figureheads" heads of state, like constitutional monarchs, and not active executive heads of government. In contrast, in a full-fledged presidential system, a President is chosen by the people to be the head of the executive branch. Presidential governments make no distinction between the positions of head of state and head of government, both of which are held by the President. Most parliamentary governments have a symbolic head of state in the form of a President or Monarch. That person is responsible for the formalities of state functions as the figurehead while the Prime Minister generally exercises the constitutional prerogatives of the head of government. Such figurehead presidents tend to be elected in a much less direct manner than active presidential systems, some are for example, elected by a vote of the legislature. A few nations, such as Ireland, do have a popularly elected ceremonial, president. A few countries (e.g., South Africa) have powerful presidents who are elected by the legislature. Countries with a pure presidential system are Kenya and USA; however, South Sudan has semi-presidential system of government.

These presidents are chosen in the same way as a prime minister, yet are heads of both state and government. These executives are titled "presidents", but are in practice similar to prime ministers. Other countries with the same system include Botswana, the Marshall Islands, and Nauru. In the United States of America, the method of a legislative vote for president was a part of Madison's Virginia Plan and was seriously considered by the framers of the American Constitution. Presidents in presidential systems are always active participants in the political process, though the extent of their relative power may be influenced by the political makeup of the legislature and whether their supporters or opponents have the dominant position therein. In some presidential systems such as Uganda, Weimar Germany, South Korea or the Republic of China (or Taiwan), there is an office of prime minister or premier but, unlike in semi-presidential or parliamentary systems, the Premier is responsible to the president rather than to the legislature.

The Features of the Presidential Executive

The chief executive or the president in the presidential democracy is mostly popularly elected. According to Gabriel Almond et al (2007), the American president is elected indirectly by the Electoral College (though actually by indirect popular) for a four-year term. The president may be from a party other than the party controlling the majority of seats in the legislature. This cannot happen in a parliamentary democracy where the leading party or coalition of parties with majority seats forms the government. When the president emerges from a party different from the one controlling the legislature, what results is called a "divided" government. The executive is separately elected and hence not a member of the legislature. The president is however elected to a fixed term. The president can only be reelected once. The president cannot dissolve the assembly but the assembly can impeach the president, if found to have abused his oath of office. The presidential system has a single executive; hence executive power is not shared between separate persons. The legislature is separated from the executive organ. No member of the legislature can serve in the executive office unless and until he has resigned his or her position in the legislature. The lower chamber is always much larger and representative than the upper chamber. However, unlike the British House of Lords, the membership of the upper chamber is always by election. Legislators are elected into a specified term of office. But in most presidential democracies, no limit is imposed on the number of time that legislators may be reelected.

The judiciary, manned largely by distinct personnel, is vested with the power of adjudication. However, unlike the constraint on the judiciary in the British model where no court can review any laws made by the assembly, in the American presidential model, the laws made by the legislature are subjected to judicial review. If such laws are found to be inconsistent with the Constitution, the laws become null and void. As Almond et al (2007) argue, the Supreme Court, through its power of judicial review, can declare any act of the President or Congress null and void on the ground that it violates the Constitution (Almond et al, 2007). However, the extent to which a nation's judiciary is free to perform its roles, and efficiently too, may depend on how developed and rooted democracy is in the state. For instance, the experience from Latin America shows that in states that are just emerging from one form of an authoritarian regime or the other, the judiciary is usually not too strong and often incapable of fully asserting its authority. This fact was demonstrated also in Nigeria, another developing African country, where the executive flagrantly violated judicial orders with impunity after Nigeria returned to democratic governance after nearly fifteen years of military dictatorship.

Although the presidential system is largely believed and accepted to have emerged on the global political scene consequent on the adoption and the design of the American Constitution of 1778, the principles inherent in the model have been accepted and practiced by most other modern states, particularly countries in the developing world. As Newton VonDeth (2005) notes, influenced by the USA, many central and South American democracies have presidential governments. The countries, which have the system, include Argentina, Bolivia, Chile, Costa Rica, the Dominic Republic, El Salvador, Mexico, Peru and Uruguay. Apart from the countries in Latin America, a good number of countries in Africa have settled for the presidential system. These countries include Niger, Benin, Botswana, Namibia, Nigeria and Kenya (VonDeth, 2005).

However, one important point to note about some of the developing countries which practice the presidential democracy is that despite predicting the system on the principles of power dispersion and checks and balances, the legislatures are most often too weak to check the executive. Helmke (2002), particularly, notes that despite the in-built checks and balances characterizing the presidential system, the separation of power in Latin America is so notoriously weak the executive holds enormous power in governance (Helmke, 2002). The president is so strong in the Niger Republic that he can dissolve the legislature and this was demonstrated in the dissolution of the assembly in Niger in August 2009. The Niger Republic Constitution was designed to subordinate the legislature to the executive in both law and policy making. The presidential system operational in Nigeria is different from the one that collapsed in Niger because the legislature in Nigeria has been equipped with sufficient power to check undue executive encroachment. The President of Niger operated with little restraint on his authority. This made him completely dominate the legislative and judiciary branches. In South Sudan, the President is so strong in that he can declare a state of emergency, dissolve the legislature and declare war.

11.7. The Semi-Presidential System of the Government

This model of government, which has its origin in the Fifth Republic Constitution of France, is characterized by a fair blend of the features of both the parliamentary and presidential systems. One of the major features of the model is the executive is elected by the people into a fixed term of office. Thus, the legitimacy of the authority exercised by the president flows from the consent given in a popular election. However, unlike the presidential arrangement, a prime minister selected from the majority party or coalition of parties in parliament work alongside the directly elected president. European examples of this model are found in France and Portugal. Under the model, federal ministers are selected from the legislature. However, where individuals that are not members of the legislature are selected or appointed as ministers, they are required to seek election in subsequent elections.

The President under the French model is more powerful than the executive under the pure presidential system of the US and Nigeria. The President of France can impose his/her will on the assembly and make it to pass legislation through the constitutional court.

The French constitution vested in the president, temporary power of dictatorship when it appears that the republic or sovereignty of the state is under threat, as well as when the functioning of public authority is interrupted. The president has certain power exclusively while he shares some power with the prime minister. Also, the Parliament of France consists of two houses, the Senate and the National Assembly. The senate is elected by indirect suffrage. The Senate is seen as representing local authorities and also constitutes the territorial assemblies of the republic. The National Assembly is directly elected by adult suffrage. For the Judiciary, the Fifth Republic constitution of France also declares that the President of the republic is the guarantor of judicial independence and authority. He is assisted by the Superior Council of the Judiciary consisting of the minister of justice and nine others nominated by the president; the council is presided over by the president of the republic. This political configuration seen in the semi-presidential system clearly undermines the principle of separation of power and in fact concentrated more power in the executive than any other organ of government.

11.8. Mixed Systems in Developing Societies

Different versions of the parliamentary-presidential mix have been adopted in the developing democracies. For instance, in Ghana, while the president is popularly elected, the bulk of the members of the cabinet are appointed from the elected members of the assembly. Unlike France, however, judicial review of the constitutionality of the actions and pronouncement of the assembly and the executive could be undertaken by the Ghanaian judiciary. In South Africa where a model close to that of Ghana is operated also, the president is elected or selected from the majority party in the lower chamber. The president is chosen from the National Assembly. Similarly, the members of the cabinet are selected from the legislature.

Advantages of the Presidential System of Government

Generally, four basic advantages of the presidential system could be outlined in every system where it is practiced. They include:

I. Direct Mandate

In a presidential system, the president is often elected directly by the people. To some, this makes the president's power more legitimate than that of a leader appointed indirectly. In the United States, the president is elected neither directly nor through the legislature, but by an electoral college. A prime minister is usually chosen by a majority of the people's representatives, while a president is usually chosen directly by the people. According to supporters of the presidential system, a popularly elected leadership is inherently more democratic than a leadership chosen by a legislative body, even if the legislative body was itself elected, to rule. By making more than one electoral choice, voters in a presidential system can more accurately indicate their policy preferences. For example, in the United States of America, some political scientists interpret the late Cold War tendency to elect a Democratic Congress and a Republican President as the choice for a Republican foreign policy and a Democratic domestic policy. It is also stated that the direct mandate of a president makes him or her more accountable. The reasoning behind this argument is that a prime minister is "shielded" from public opinion by the apparatus of the state, being several steps removed. Critics of this view note, however, that presidents cannot typically be removed from power when their policies no longer reflect the wishes of the citizenry. In the United States, presidents can only be removed by an impeachment trial for high crimes and misdemeanors, whereas prime ministers can typically be removed if they fail a motion of confidence in their government.

II. Separation of Powers

A presidential system establishes the presidency and the legislature as two parallel structures. Supporters claim that this arrangement allows each structure to supervise the other, preventing abuses. The fact that a presidential system separates the executive from the legislature is sometimes held up as an advantage, in that each branch may scrutinize the actions of the other. In a parliamentary system, the executive is drawn from the legislature, making criticism of one by the other considerably less likely. A formal condemnation of the executive by the legislature is often regarded to be a vote of no confidence. According to supporters of the presidential system, the lack of checks and balances means that misconduct by a prime minister may never be discovered. Critics respond that if the president's party controls a presidential system's legislature, the same situation exists. Proponents note that even in such a situation a legislator from the president's party is in a better position to criticize the president or his policies should he deem it necessary, since a president is immune to the effects of a motion of no confidence. In parliamentary systems, party discipline is much more strictly enforced. If a parliamentary backbencher publicly criticizes the executive or its policies to any significant extent then he/she faces a much higher prospect of losing his/her party's nomination, or even outright expulsion from the party.

Despite the existence of the no-confidence vote, in practice, it is extremely difficult to stop a prime minister or cabinet that has made its decision. In a parliamentary system, if important legislation proposed by the incumbent prime minister and his cabinet is "voted down" by a majority of the members of parliament then it is considered to be a vote of no-confidence. The incumbent government must then either resign or call elections to be held, a consequence few backbenchers are willing to endure. Hence, a no confidence vote in some parliamentary countries, like Britain, only occurs a few times in a century.

III. Speed and Decisiveness

Some argue that a president with strong powers can usually enact changes quickly. However, others argue that the separation of powers slows the system down. Also, some proponents of the presidential system claim that the system can respond more rapidly to emerging situations than to parliamentary ones. A prime minister, when taking action, needs to retain the support of the legislature, but a president is often less constrained. Other supporters of presidential systems sometimes argue in the exact opposite direction, however, saying that presidential systems can slow decision-making to beneficial ends. Divided government, where different parties control the presidency and the legislature, is said to restrain the excesses of both parties, and guarantee bipartisan input into legislation.

IV. Stability

A president, by virtue of a fixed term, may provide more stability than a prime minister who can be dismissed at any time. Although most parliamentary governments go long periods without a no-confidence vote, Italy, Israel, and the French Fourth Republic have all experienced difficulties maintaining stability. When parliamentary systems have multiple parties and governments are forced to rely on coalitions, as they do in nations that use a system of proportional representation, extremist parties can theoretically use the threat of leaving a coalition to further their agendas.

Many people consider presidential systems to be more able to survive emergencies. A country under enormous stress may, supporters argue, be better off being led by a president with a fixed term than rotating premierships. France during the Algerian controversy switched to a semi-presidential system as did Sri Lanka during its civil war, while Israel experimented with a directly elected prime minister in 1992. In France and Sri Lanka, the results are widely considered to have been positive. However, in the case of Israel, an unprecedented proliferation of smaller parties occurred-leading to the restoration of the previous system of selecting a prime minister.

The fact that elections are fixed in a presidential system is considered to be a welcome "check" on the powers of the executive, contrasting parliamentary systems, which often allow the prime minister to call elections whenever he sees fit, or orchestrate his own vote of no confidence to trigger an election when he cannot get a legislative item passed. The presidential model is said to discourage this sort of opportunism, and instead force the executive to operate within the confines of a term he cannot alter to suit his own needs. Theoretically, if a president's positions and actions have had a positive impact on their respective country, then it is likely that their party's candidate (possibly they) will be elected for another term in office.

Disadvantages of the Presidential System of Government
Generally, three basic disadvantages of the presidential system have been identified by scholars. They are:

I. Tendency Towards Authoritarianism

Winning the presidency is a winner-take-all, zero-sum prize. A prime minister who does not enjoy a majority in the legislature will have to either form a coalition or, if he is able to lead a minority government, govern in a manner acceptable to at least some of the opposition parties. Even if the prime minister leads a majority government, he must still govern within (perhaps unwritten) constraints as determined by the members of his party - a premier in this situation is often at greater risk of losing his party leadership than his party is at risk of losing the next election. On the other hand, once elected a president can not only marginalize the influence of other parties, but can exclude rival factions in his own party as well, or even leave the party whose ticket he was elected under. The president can thus rule without any allies for the duration of one or possibly multiple terms, a worrisome situation for many interest groups. Juan Linz and Stephen Andrew (1996) argue as follows:

> The danger that zero-sum presidential elections pose is compounded by the rigidity of the president's fixed term in office. Winners and losers are sharply defined for the entire period of the presidential mandate... losers must wait four or five years without any access to executive power and patronage. The zero-sum game in presidential regimes raises the stakes of presidential elections and inevitably exacerbates their attendant tension and polarization. Constitutions that only require plurality support are said to be especially undesirable, as significant power can be vested in a person who does not enjoy support from a majority of the population. Some political scientists go further, and argue that presidential systems have difficulty sustaining democratic practices, noting that presidentialism has slipped into authoritarianism in many of

the countries in which it has been implemented (Linz & Stephen, 1996).

Lipset et al (1955) are careful to point out that this has taken place in political cultures not conducive to democracy and that militaries have tended to play a prominent role in most of these countries (Lipset, et al, 1955). Nevertheless, certain aspects of the presidential system may have played a role in some situations. In a presidential system, the legislature and the president have equally valid mandates from the public. There is often no way to the reconcile conflict between the branches of government. When the president and legislature are in disagreement and the government is not working effectively, there is a powerful incentive to employ extra-constitutional maneuvers to break the deadlock. Ecuador is sometimes presented as a case study of democratic failures over the past quarter-century. Presidents have ignored the legislature or bypassed it altogether. Once President had the National Assembly tear-gassed, while paratroopers kidnapped another who agreed to certain congressional demands.

From 1979 through 1988, Ecuador staggered through a succession of executive-legislative confrontations that created a near-permanent crisis atmosphere in the policy. In 1984, President León Febres Cordero tried to physically bar new congressionally appointed Supreme Court appointees from taking their seats. In Brazil, presidents have accomplished their objectives by creating executive agencies over which Congress had no say. It should be noted that this alleged authoritarian tendency is often best seen in unitary states that have presidential systems. Federal states, with multiple states (or provincial) governments that are semi-sovereign, provide additional checks on authoritarian tendencies. This can be seen in the United States, where there are fifty states, each semi-sovereign, each having its own three branch elected government (governor, legislature, and court system), police, emergency response system, and military force. If an extreme extra-constitutional action, such as the President dissolving Congress, occurred within the Federal government of the United States, it would not necessarily result in the President being able to rule dictatorially since he or she would have to deal with the fifty state governments.

II. Separation of Powers

Even though it has been acknowledged as an instrument of check and balance, critics of the presidential system believe that the system does not offer voters the kind of accountability seen in parliamentary systems. It is easy for either the president or Congress to escape blame by blaming the other. Describing the United States, for instance, former Treasury Secretary C. Douglas Dillon said the president blames Congress, the Congress blames the president, and the public remains confused and disgusted with government in Washington. But appropriate constitutional safeguards, especially in terms of adequate provisions that spell out the powers, duties and obligations of each of these institutions or offices is a way out of such lacuna, where it indeed exists.

III. Impediments to Leadership Change

Another problem of presidentialism is that it is often difficult to remove a president from office early. The procedure is often long, arduous and cumbersome. In most countries, it is also marred by political colorations. Even if a president is proved to be inefficient, even if he becomes unpopular, even if his policy is unacceptable to the majority of his countrymen, he and his methods must be endured until the moment comes for a new election. Consider John Tyler, who only became president because William Henry Harrison had died after thirty days. Tyler refused to sign Whig legislation, was loathed by his nominal party, but remained firmly in control of the executive branch. Since the legal way to remove an unpopular president is often unrealizable, many presidential countries have experienced military coups to remove a leader who is said to have lost his mandate. In parliamentary systems, unpopular leaders can be quickly removed by a vote of no confidence, a procedure which is reckoned to be a "pressure release valve" for political tension. Votes of no confidence are easier to achieve in minority government situations, but even if the unpopular leader heads a majority government, nonetheless, he is often in a far less secure position than a president. Removing a president through impeachment is a process mandated by the constitution and is usually made into a very difficult process. By comparison, the process of removing a party leader is governed by the (often much less formal) rules of the party in question.

Nearly all parties (including governing parties) have a relatively simple and straightforward process for removing their leaders. If a premier sustains a serious enough blow to his/her popularity and refuses to resign on his/her own prior to the next election, then members of his/her party face the prospect of losing their seats. So other prominent party members have a very strong incentive to initiate a leadership challenge in hopes of mitigating damage to the party. More often than not, a premier facing a serious challenge will resolve to save face by resigning before he/she is formally removed-Prime Minister Margaret Thatcher's relinquishing of her premiership being a prominent example.

Finally, many have criticized presidential systems for their alleged slowness in responding to their citizens' needs. Often, the checks and balances make action extremely difficult. Walter Bagehot said of the American system the executive is crippled by not getting the law it needs, and the legislature is spoiled by having to act without responsibility: the executive becomes unfit for its name, since it cannot execute what it decides on; the legislature is demoralized by liberty, by taking decisions of others (and not itself) will suffer the effects. Defenders of presidential systems, on the other hand, hold that this can serve to ensure that minority wishes and rights are not trampled upon, thus preventing a "tyranny of the majority" and vice versa protecting the wishes and rights of the majority from abuse by the legislature and/ or executive that holds a contrary view point, especially when there are frequent, scheduled elections. British-Irish philosopher and MP Edmund Burke stated that officials should be elected based on his (or her) unbiased opinion, his (or her) mature judgment, (and) his (or her) enlightened conscience and therefore should reflect on the arguments for and against certain policies before taking positions and then act out on what an official would believe to be best in the long run for one's constituents and country as a whole even if it means short term backlash. Thus, defenders of presidential systems hold that sometimes what is wisest may not always be the most popular decision and vice versa.

11.9. Differences between Parliamentary and Presidential Systems of Government

A number of key theoretical differences exist between a presidential and a parliamentary system:

I. The Principle of Presidential System

The central principle is that the legislative and executive branches of government should be separate. This leads to the separate election of a president, who is elected to office for a fixed term, and only removable for gross misdemeanor by impeachment and dismissal. In addition, he or she does not need to choose cabinet members commanding the support of the legislature. By contrast, in a parliamentary system, the executive branch is led by a council of ministers, headed by a Prime Minister, who is directly accountable to the legislature and often has their background in the legislature (regardless of whether it is called a "parliament", a "diet", or a "chamber"). In parliamentary systems of government, the legislature is formally supreme and appoints a member from its house as the prime minister, which acts as the executive. In the separation of powers doctrine, the legislature in a presidential system is considered a power branch that is coequal to and independent of the both judiciary and the executive. In addition to enacting laws, legislatures usually have exclusive authority to raise taxes and adopt the budget and other money bills.

II. President's Set Term of Office

The legislature also exists for a set term of office and cannot be dissolved ahead of schedule in a presidential system. By contrast, in parliamentary systems, the legislature can typically be dissolved at any stage during its life by the head of state, usually on the advice of either the Prime Minister alone, by the Prime Minister and cabinet, or by the cabinet. The primary components of a legislature are one or more chambers or houses: assemblies that debate and vote upon bills. A legislature with only one house is called unicameral. A bicameral legislature possesses two separate chambers, usually described as an upper house and a lower house, which often differ in duties, powers, and the methods used for the selection of members. Much focus has been on tri-cameral legislatures; the most recent existed in the waning years of white-minority rule in South Africa.

III. In Most Parliamentary Systems

The lower house is the more powerful house while the upper house is merely a chamber of advice or review. However, in presidential systems, the powers of the two houses are often similar or equal. In federations, it is typical for the upper house to represent the component states; the same applies to the supranational legislature of the European Union. For this purpose, the upper house may either contain the delegates of state governments, as is the case in the European Union and in Germany and was the case in the United States before 1913, or be elected according to a formula that grants equal representation to states with smaller populations, as is the case in Australia and the modern United States.

IV. In a Presidential System

The president usually has special privileges in the enactment of the legislation, namely, the possession of the power of veto over legislation of bills, in some cases subject to the power of the legislature by weighed majority to override the veto. However, it is extremely rare for the president to have the power to directly propose laws, or cast a vote on legislation. The legislature and the president are thus expected to serve as checks and balances on each other's powers.

V. Presidential System Presidents

It may also be given a great deal of constitutional authority in the exercise of the office of Commander-in-Chief, a constitutional title given to most presidents. In addition, the presidential power to receive ambassadors as head of state is usually interpreted as giving the president broad powers to conduct foreign policy. Though semi-presidential systems may reduce a president's power over day-to-day government affairs, semi-presidential systems commonly give the president power over foreign policy.

VI. Presidential Systems also Have Fewer Ideological Parties than Parliamentary Systems

Sometimes in the United States, the policies preferred by the two parties have been very similar. In some developing countries, differences between political parties are only in terms of personality, and perhaps the ethnic background of political parties, as elections are rarely fought or won on issues.

Overlapping Elements of both Parliamentary and Presidential Systems

However, in practice, elements of both systems overlap. Though a president in a presidential system does not have to choose a government answerable to the legislature, the legislature may have the right to scrutinize his or her appointments to high governmental office, with the right, on some occasions, to block an appointment. In the United States and Nigeria, for example, the Senate must confirm many appointments. By contrast, though answerable to parliament, a parliamentary system's cabinet may be able to make use of the parliamentary 'whip' (an obligation on party members in parliament to vote with their party) to control and dominate parliament, reducing parliament's ability to control the government. Some countries, such as France have similarly evolved to such a degree that they can no longer be accurately described as either presidential or parliamentary-style governments, and are instead grouped under the category of semi-presidential or hybrid.

11.10. Comparing the British and American Systems (Models)

The presidential system of the United States and the parliamentary system of Britain share some characteristics and differ in many other respects. The two case studies are being assessed along the following parameters

I. The Legislature

The primary purpose of a legislature in any constitutional democracy is to enact laws. However, the specific institutional environment in which this is done differs in a significant way from one type of system to another. In fact, the most fundamental difference is one of principle i.e., the principle of parliamentary sovereignty. This major principle distinguishes Britain from most other democratic countries. Parliament may enact any law it likes and no other body can set the law aside on the grounds that it is unconstitutional or undesirable. Conversely, the American system places the Constitution above even the congress. Despite these fundamental differences, certain functions performed by the legislative branches under both systems are essentially the same, for example, either congressional or parliamentary approval is required to legitimize any new law. Also, both legislatures serve as forums in which political, economic, and social issues are debated. Both Congress and Parliament represent the true symbols of representative democracy.

II. Legislative Independence

Although the powers of congress are limited by the Constitution, US legislatures have far more latitude than their British counterpart. Parliament is normally bicameral, but real legislature power is concentrated in the members of the House of Commons. The prime minister and cabinet usually do not make policy without first consulting influential MPs, and cabinet domination of parliament is strictly supported by party discipline. Congress presents an entirely different picture. Both its 435-member House and its 100-member Senate are powerful bodies whose consent is necessary before any measure can be enacted into law. In addition, representatives and senators tend to be locally oriented rather than national constituencies. They are elected to promote local interests and have the freedom to vote accordingly.

III. Legislative Predictability

The greater independence called legislators under the presidential system makes Congress a much more unpredictable institution than its British counterpart. In Britain, a party that wins a national election by a clear mandate is presumed to have a popular mandate to carry out its campaign promises. Although disagreement may arise within the ranks of the governing party, the general tone and direction of the government are usually clear before Parliament. US election is different in many ramifications in this respect. Even in presidential election years when the presidency and vice-presidency, one-third of senate seats, and all House seats are contested, no clear national consensus may emerge. It is also possible that no legislative consensus will emerge, for instance, the newly elected president is not skilled in dealing with Congress. Generally speaking, legislative results from a give-and-take process involving both houses of Congress as well as the White House.

IV. Structural Complexity

In Congress, there is a fragmentation of authority and power, which makes its structure notably more complex than that of the British Parliament. There are six significant standing committees in the entire House of Commons. These committees are not even specialized; their twenty to fifty members consider bills without reference to the subject matter. They lack the power to call hearings or solicit expert testimony, they cannot table a bill, and at best they can make technical adjustments in its language. In summary, committees' work in parliament is unexciting and uneventful. By contrast, the parliament committee system of the U.S congress has no less than fifteen specialized committees. These committees have a number of subcommittees, with each charged with even more specialized tasks. In addition, committees and subcommittees have the power to hold hearing and summon witnesses as part of routine investigations into executive branch programme and operations.

V. Watchdog Role

The Congress performs a watchdog role, which takes various shapes. Policy reviews can occur at any point in the legislative process (during the authorization and appropriation phases of the budgetary process, for example, by means of investigations and hearings). The British parliamentary system stands in sharp contrast to this.

VI. The Executive-Legislative Nexus

Another key difference between the two political systems lies in the extent to which the legislature is involved in determining the composition of the executive branch. In a parliamentary system, parliament plays a key role in determining the composition of a new administration (the cabinet). The prime minister heads the majority party in parliament, and the cabinet comprises of parliament leaders. In fact, the parliamentary system blurs the distinctions between the legislature and executive powers; it is often difficult to determine where the authority of one branch starts and that of the other ends.

This fusion of power is not the case under the presidential system of government. Unlike senators and representatives, natural majorities elect presidents and the presidency derives its powers from a separate section of the Constitution. Although Congress does have some influence through the ratification of executive nominees.

CHAPTER TWELVE

12.1. Comparative Hydropolitics

12.2. Concept of Hydro-Politics

Hydropolitics has recently appeared as a very vital branch of comparative politics because of the greatest interest that has been put on water resources in the world. Hydropolitics refers to as the geopolitics of water that involves struggling over the control of water resources by the countries in the world (Waterbury, 1979). The concept of Hydropolitics was first introduced in a book of John Waterbury in 1979. Hydro refers to water and politic refers to interest and influence. Thus, Hydropolitics is defined as the politics of water (Waterbury, 1979). Most people take water for granted. It rarely came to mind that water had political and economic value which, in today's circumstances, is now overwhelming its social value.

In early 1990s and mid-2000s, the concept of hydro-politics was further expounded by other critical scholars of the water resources politics. In reviewing of the empirical literature, the concept was applied to analyse conflict and cooperation in several trans-boundary river basins mostly in poor countries, particularly, in Sub-Saharan Africa (Zeitoun, 2010). Peter Mollinga (2008) describes four domains of water politics research: a) everyday politics b) national water politics c) interstate hydro-politics and d) global water politics (Mollinga, 2008).

To understand the importance of water issues and the links between water and politics, a brief overview of the world water situation is in order. Water covers around seventy percent of the earth. Fresh water constitutes less than three percent of the world's total water. Two-thirds of that fresh water is locked in glaciers and polar ice caps. Most of the remaining water resides in soil and underground aquifers. Thus, approximately, 0.01 percent of all water is accessible to the human population. Still, at the present time, water exists in abundance. If the fresh and sea waters were spread evenly, they would cover the globe to a height of two thousand seven hundred meters. Similarly, the three percent of fresh water, which constitutes the bulk of our supply, would still make a layer of seventy meters high if it were spread evenly (Turton, 2000).

Between 1850 and 1990, the world population doubled while water use grew 300 percent. During the past seventy years alone the world population grew by more than three billion people: from 2.6 billion in 1950 to over nine billion in 2020. According to Michael Klare (2002), "if this rate of increase persists, we will soon be using 100 percent of the world's available supply probably by the mid-22nd century" (Klare, 2002). To complicate matters, water is a source of inequality both in terms of distribution and of consumption. With twenty two percent of the world's population, China accounts for seven percent of its renewable freshwater; Canada, with a half percent of the world's population, accounts for 9 percent of the world's renewable fresh water (Ibid). Just ten countries hold more than half the fresh water available on the planet. Meanwhile, global population growth is heavily concentrated in those areas of the world North Africa, the Middle East and South Asia, where the supply of water is already proving inadequate for many human needs" (Ezbakhe & Brehaut, 2021). Within the next twenty-five years, one-third of the world's population will experience severe water scarcity.

It is helpful to know that water scarce-countries are defined as those with less than one thousand cubic meters available per person per year, and water-stressed ones as those with less than five hundred cubic meters per person per year (Ibid, 2021). The discrepancy between the extremes aforementioned constitutes what may be termed a structure of water-based global apartheid. In such a global inequality and the local challenges, it engenders, the potential for water-based transnational conflicts should be taken seriously. The urgency of this situation can be explained by the fact that there are one hundred and sixty-five trans-border rivers worldwide. Their basins cover fifty percent of the landmass and thirty-two percent of borders are made of water. About forty percent of the world's population is living in river basins shared by many countries. In view of the global climate change and the anticipated alteration of precipitation patterns that will entail, the potential for water-based hardship and water-based conflict is likely to increase in many regions. Perhaps most prominent are the Middle East around the Tigris and the Euphrates River basins and northeast Africa in the Nile River basin.

12.3. Characteristics of Hydro States

Hydro-States are States that are consumed by the politics of water. They have some characteristics, which are important and should be discussed in this book. The following are the characteristics of these Hydro-States:

1. **Poverty Ridden.** Most of Hydro-States are very poor countries. From China to Thailand, North Korea, Philippines, Indonesia, Egypt, Sudan, Eritrea, Ethiopia, South Sudan, Uganda etc., these countries have low GDP per capita. Although some of these countries have a growing GDP per capita, the trickle-down effect is limited.

2. **Post-Colonial.** The majority of Hydro-States are former colonies of the great powers. All the above-named countries except Ethiopia were colonized by various great Western and Eastern powers and continued to be influenced by the former colonial policies.

3. **Conflict Perennial.** We have seen countries such as China, North Korea, Sudan, Egypt, South Sudan, Ethiopia and Uganda drawn into conflicts. Tension over the South China Sea poses a significant risk of conflict with China. China, Taiwan, Vietnam, Malaysia, Brunei, and the Philippines have competing territorial and jurisdictional claims, particularly over rights to exploit the region's possibly extensive reserves of oil and gas.

4. **Border Disputes**: As already seen with China on jurisdictional claims over the South China Sea, borders disputes are common with Hydro-States. Countries such as North Korea, Egypt, Sudan, South Sudan, Ethiopia, Eritrea, and Uganda also have unresolved border disputes.

5. **Developing Economies:** All the Hydro-States except China and North Korea are developing countries. Indeed, most of them are middle- and lower-income economies.

6. **Kleptocrats**: All the Hydro-States are run by bunch of juntas and newly emerged & decorated authoritarian leaders. Public decisions are personalized and the leaders are notoriously corrupt, abusers of human rights and ruled with impunity.

12.4. Common Differences Amongst Nile Basin Initiative (NBI) Countries

The Nile Basin Initiative (NBI) is a partnership among the Nile Riparian States that "seeks to develop the river in a cooperative manner, share substantial socioeconomic benefits and promote regional peace and security" (Swain, 2002). It was formally launched in February 1999 by the water ministers of nine countries that share the river - Egypt, Sudan, Ethiopia, Uganda, Kenya, Tanzania, Burundi, Rwanda, and the Democratic Republic of Congo (DRC), with Eritrea as an observer. South Sudan joined the partnership in 2011.

Common Differences among NBI Countries

NBI countries are considered to be different from one another on 8 broad categories:

1. **Size of the Country**. A country can be large in terms of its physical size, its population or by the level of its national income. So NBIs have differences in physical size, population and national income. For instance, while the DRC is the large in the size; Egypt is the most populous nation.

2. **Historical Background**. It is important to understand the colonial background of a country. Colonial rule usually has a significant influence on the pre-existing institutions and culture of a country. Some of these influences may have been helpful but others were very harmful. Once colonial rule ended, it took a long time for the newly independent country to find its own foothold. Therefore, it is very important to understand if a country has colonial history of country and when and how it became independent.

3. **Physical and Human Resources.** The number of physical resources, which include land, minerals and other raw materials available to a country can make a huge difference in the life cycle of its population. The countries in the Nile Basin differ very much in terms of their human resources. Some countries may have a small but highly skilled educated and innovative population. While some countries may have a very large but (mainly) a very low skill population with very little or no education at all. Yet, there can be countries, which may have large population with average to high levels of skill and education. Egypt and Kenya both have high skill workforces.

4. **Ethnic and Religious Composition**. The more diverse a country is, in terms of ethnic and religious composition, the more will be internal strife and political instability. This internal strife and political instability can lead to violent conflicts and even self-destructive wars that waste of valuable resources which could have been used to promote valuable development goals. Sudan, DRC, Ethiopia,

Uganda, Kenya, and Tanzania are highly diverse. However, it is Tanzania that has kept its ethnic and religious peace. This is because Tanzania has a strong leadership foundation built by late Mwalimu Julius Nyerere which has promoted ethnic diversity and cohesion.

5. **Relative Importance of Public and Private Sectors**. The relative importance and size of public and private sector vary a lot in the NBI countries. Countries that have severe shortage of skilled human resources tend to have large public sectors and state-owned enterprises. This is on the assumption that limited skilled manpower cannot compete well in the private sector. The widespread failure of a number of countries with large public sectors raises questions regarding the validity of these claims. Economic policies to promote the same development objectives would be different in countries with different compositions of public and private sectors. Egypt, Kenya and Ethiopia are large economies while Uganda, Rwanda, Tanzania and South Sudan are small economies.

6. **Industrial Structure**. NBI countries also differ a lot in terms of the size and quality of their industrial structure. The size and type of an industrial sector depend on the policies adopted in the past, which again may have a lot to do with the history of the country. Egypt, Sudan, Ethiopia and Kenya have solid industrial capabilities while Uganda, Tanzania and Rwanda have growing industrial capabilities. Burundi and South Sudan have no any industrial capacity.

7. **External Dependence.** External dependence can be economic, political or cultural in nature. NBI countries being mostly small and underdeveloped have to depend a lot on developed countries for trade, technology and training. The extent of dependence varies amongst countries and is influenced by the size, history and location of the country. Sudan, South Sudan, Burundi and DRC are mostly surviving on foreign aid due to the way violent conflict has devastated their economies.

8. **Political Structure, Power and Interest Groups.** NBI countries also vary in terms of the political system and structure, the size of the vested interest group and its influence on the political power structure. Although interest groups are seen to be present in every society to a greater extent than in other countries. A small and powerful elite rule most NBI countries directly or indirectly. Effective social and economic change thus requires that either elite groups be enlisted for support or more powerful democratic forces offset the power of the elite.

12.5. Theories of Hydro-Politics

Theory of Treaty Succession

Advanced by Valerie Knobelsdorf (1999), the issue of treaty succession has played a central role in debates about modern water governance, particularly; Nile has served as a basis for the refutation of the Agreements by some upper riparian states (Knobelsdorf, 1999). In the cases of Ethiopia, Tanzania and Kenya, national leaders have directly refused to be bound by the 1929 and 1959 Agreements, arguing that these were signed on their nations' behalf and without their consultations (Kliot, 1998). As such, there exists a question as to whether treaty obligations are legally passed from the colonized to the independent states. However, succession manoeuvres exist and these nations have made such statements primarily to reserve a future claim to water for development, generally lacking the need or capacity to utilize the river for irrigation purposes, which would be the largest potential draw on Nile water. Some of the upper riparian States, including Uganda and Rwanda, have not yet taken a firm stance on the validity of the 1959 Agreement. Resources excess and lack of capacity have generally prevented the need for some countries to take a solid stance on the issue, although growing water scarcity and newly proposed development projects have begun to change this. Kenya, Uganda and Tanzania, for example, have recently shown their interest in developing small and medium scale irrigation projects around Lake Victoria and some international disagreements have arisen about the rights of local fishermen in the lake and the succession juxtaposition over water control continues. A successful Nile Waters Agreement will likely respond to the lessons learned under the colonially-imposed Agreements. The complexity of interests in the Nile region calls for autochthonous solutions that build on localized expertise and community concerns. Although some elements of existing and proposed regimes might prove to be helpful elements in a future agreement, only a specifically tailored approach to Nile governance will be able to address regional priorities while avoiding the "substantial mismatch" of a colonial legal transplant into a unique and complex situation (Knobelsdorf, 1999).

Theory of Territorial Sovereignty

Advanced by Eric W. Sievers, the theory of territorial sovereignty is central to transboundary claims to international freshwater bodies (Sievers, 2011). In the governance of land, the issue of territorial sovereignty can be very simple: a sovereign nation generally has the right to exert exclusive and unrestricted jurisdiction over land territory within its boundaries. With ambient resources such as water, and especially with the emergence of modern environmental law, this absolute approach to territorial sovereignty becomes more complicated. As in common law property ownership, the law's consideration of ambient resources does not fit easily into broadly established frameworks. Under the theory of absolute territorial sovereignty, the waters flowing through the boundaries of a nation are within the complete domain of that nation, which can use them in any manner with no regard for downstream beneficiaries. The former Iraqi government, for example, operated under this approach, justifying its use of the Euphrates River based on its absolute right to do with the water as it pleases (Sultana, 2019).

Although this theory is usually moderated by international diplomatic concerns or developmental capacity limitations, it is often adopted in times of extreme need, such as widespread drought or war, or in developing countries seeking to utilize all available resources. Among the Nile's basin nations, Rwanda and Ethiopia have most often supported this type of approach, stating that sovereign states have the unconditional right to waters originating or flowing within their borders. This assertion is made stronger by the fact that Ethiopia also serves as the primary catchment area for a majority of the Blue Nile waters, increasing the territorial attachment to the river's flow within the nation. Although international adherence to the doctrine of absolute territorial sovereignty is waning, especially in the allocation of ambient resources, it has been historically upheld in a number of instances. The famous Lake Lanoux Arbitration between France and Spain before the International Court of Justice (ICJ), for example, notes that limitations on territorial integrity are unusual, with judicial decisions recognizing treaty restrictions only where there is clear and convincing evidence… especially when they impair the territorial sovereignty of a state. Under this rule, if the doctrine of absolute territorial sovereignty is adopted in the Nile Basin, it could be limited only by a valid, binding and explicit agreement between sovereign nations.

12.6. Analysis of Nile Water Treaties Signed, 1891, 1906, 1929, 1959, 1993

The Nile River Basin and Treaties

The Nile River is the longest river in the world. Running through 6,695 km, the Nile is a major transboundary water in the globe (Tedla, 2013). The Nile River Basin is a confluence of the Blue Nile stemming from Lake Tana in Ethiopia and the White Nile, stemming from Lake Victoria in Uganda. The Ethiopian waters constitute by far the greater share of the Nile. The Nile and its tributaries flow through eleven countries, Burundi, DRC, Egypt, Eritrea, Ethiopia, Kenya, Rwanda, South Sudan, Sudan, Tanzania, and Uganda. The Basin is home to different people and cultures, and over 350 million people live around it. The fact that the Nile water is the lifeblood for these people makes the cooperation and interactions among the riparian countries complex.

In terms of jurisdiction and development, the Nile has been cited as one of the few international river basins with legal arrangements for sharing the waters, and has at times been portrayed as a possible model for other international river basins. With regards to the use of the River Nile, there is a huge imbalance as the lower riparian countries utilize the most of it and the upstream countries that remained arms-crossed for centuries due to various factors such as the level of economic development and political will. At the very beginning of the twenty-first century, Ethiopia uses less than one percent of the Nile basin waters, while Egypt uses 80 percent. According to the World Bank in 1997 report, the waters of the Nile probably constitute Ethiopia's greatest natural asset for development (WB Report, 1997).

During the last decade of the 19th century and in the first two decades of the 20th century, the colonial powers negotiated among themselves over the Nile waters in the spirit of the Berlin Conference of 1884–85. But none of these negotiations took any cognizance of the inherent security, rights and interests of the basin countries themselves.

1. The 1891 Anglo-Italian Protocol

In terms of the 1891 Anglo-Italian Protocol, Great Britain and Italy demarcated their 'respective spheres of influence in North-Eastern Africa' (Tedla, 2013). This agreement allowed the UK to maintain control over the headwaters of the Tekeze (Atbara) River. Article III of this Protocol sought to protect the Egyptian interest in the Nile waters contributed by the Atbara River, the upper reaches of which fell within the newly acquired Italian possession of Eritrea. The Article is provided as follows:

"The Government of Italy undertakes not to construct on the Atbara any irrigation or other works which might sensibly modify its flow into the Nile" (Obengo, 2016).

2. The 1906 Tripartite Agreement between Great Britain, the State of Congo, France and Italy

On May 9, 1906, the United Kingdom and the Independent State of the Congo concluded a Treaty to Re-define their respective spheres of influence in Eastern and Central Africa. Article III of the Treaty provided:

"The Government of the Independent State of Congo undertakes not to construct or allow to be constructed any work over or near the Semliki or Isango Rivers, which would diminish the volume of water entering Lake Albert, except in agreement with the Sudanese Government" (Knobelsdorf, 1999).

On April 3, 1906, the UK, France and Italy secretly signed a tripartite agreement for irrigation in the most controversial of all the Nile Water agreements ceding all all Nile basin interests completely to the British. According to Andrea Batstone (1959), it is the dominating feature of legal relationships concerning the distribution and utilization of the Nile waters today (Batstone, 1959). Luke Godana (1985) adds that the agreement has become the basis of all subsequent water allocations (but) has been viewed differently by various writers" (Godana, 1985).

3. The Anglo-Egyptian Agreement of 1929

After the formal independence of Egypt had been recognized by the United Kingdom in 1922, the High Commissioner of Great Britain in Cairo, in an Exchange of Note with the Chairman of the Council of Ministers of Egypt recognized the "historical and natural rights" of Egypt over the Nile waters (Gamal, 2015). None of the upstream riparian nations was even mentioned or considered in this assertion of presumptive 'rights. Not even Ethiopia – at that time, long independent of foreign rule - was consulted or briefed in this comprehensive assumption of rights between Britain and Egypt. Since all the other countries that should rightly have been consulted about this far - reaching agreement were still under colonial rule, they were given no say whatsoever over the water resources that the Nile conferred on them because of their proximity to its waters.

4. The Egyptian-Sudanese Agreement of 1959

The negotiation process that culminated in the 1959 Agreement for the full utilization of the Nile Waters was stimulated in the 1940s when the Sudanese rejected the 1929 Anglo-Egyptian agreement that allowed the Sudan to use only what was 'left over' once Egypt's needs had been fully satisfied. Various Sudanese politicians persisted in demanding a modification of the 1929 Agreement, which was widely perceived by the Sudanese as being too restrictive of the Sudan's obvious claims to fair usage of the water of the Nile (Abdalla, 1971). According to this agreement, only Egypt and Sudan were legally recognized for the use and ownership of the Nile waters. In terms of the agreement Egypt would be allocated a lion's share of the available 55.5 billion cubic of the water while Sudan was to be allocated 18.5 billion cubic.

5. The 1993 Framework for General Cooperation between Egypt and Ethiopia

Signed in 1993 in Cairo between Egypt and Ethiopia, it was the first bilateral framework for cooperation regarding the Nile issues after the colonial period. It was signed by the late Ethiopian prime minister Meles Zenawi and former Egyptian President Hosni Mubarak. The framework stipulated those future negotiations between the two countries concerning the utilization of the waters of the Nile would be based on the rules and principles of international law.

6. Aswan High Dam and Egypt Conviction

This high rated dam by the Egypt government has a storage capacity of 164 bcm and a surface area of four thousand square kilometers. Since, it was completed, the dam became one km wide at the base, with a crest height of 111 meters. The length of the crest was 3,6 km and was 40 meters wide (Waterbury, 1979). The High Dam power station generated 6.6 billion kWh with an additional 2 billion kWh coming from the Old Aswan and nearly 5 billion kWh coming from thermal generators (Waterbury, 1979). The installed capacity is 10 billion kWh.

At the opening ceremony, Sadat's official speech castigated the USA by saying that America's broken promise of 1956 is neither the first nor will it be the last. And Soviet support in building the High Dam is neither the first nor will it be the last, for it is an expression of aspirations for freedom and peace for peoples eager for them and who resist colonialist exploitation and imperial subjugation. America's broken promise is but one link in an unending chain that leaves us no alternative but to believe it represents a political plan designed to thwart the aspirations of the Arab people. For each of America's broken promises "O my brethren - there is a Soviet promise fulfilled or on its way to fulfillment; in every sphere of hope and work; in industry, in land reclamation, in electrification, in armaments, in training, in unconditional and unlimited diplomatic support. For the Soviet Union is confident that its stance is one of defense of liberty and defense of peace" (Waterbury, 1979).

Official Egyptian figures on the performance of the Aswan High Dam show annual losses of 11.4 bcm, with 9.4 bcm being attributed to evaporation and the remaining 2 bcm being ascribed to seepage. This seems implausible against the figures that were released by Taher Abu Wafa and Aziz Hanna Labib (senior officials in the High Dam Authority) which show a vertical seepage loss of 48bcm in the first eight-year period until the substrate was saturated, followed by 6 bcm thereafter. In addition to this, 1 bcm losses were taking place horizontally. Thus, according to these two officials, in recent years one would anticipate at least 5 bcm seepage loss over and above the evaporation losses (Waterbury, 1979). Thus, the official loss figures were being underreported by around 14.4 bcm (9.4 bcm "official" evaporation loss and five bcm seepage loss). In sum, more than half of Egypt's incremental gain from the construction of the Aswan High Dam will be lost in storage (Waterbury, 1979).

Hydroelectric power station installed at the Aswan High Dam had an installed capacity of 10 billion kWh annually from twelve Russian turbines. This ignored the fact that both head and flow rates varied. This in turn is governed by other factors, the most important of which is matching the competing needs of electricity generation and irrigation. The bottom line is that rate of release and available head are not synonymous. It is common practice to minimize water release in January and February when agricultural demands are low so that drainage and irrigation canals can be cleared and maintained. This lasts for forty days with daily releases down to 85-90 mcm. This means that the turbines cannot function at capacity and with industrial demands high, this period has been reduced to twenty-one days during which 3bcm are released to satisfy non-agricultural demands. With the releases being determined largely by the agricultural sector, the level of electricity generation is often insufficient, although the installed capacity exists. The tradeoff between the two is highly complex (Waterbury, 1979). As a result, the most power that both the Old Aswan Dam and the Aswan High Dam generate together is 9 billion kWh, of which the Old Dam's share is two billion. A 1966 study claimed that on average the High Dam power station would generate 5.7 billion kWh a year (Waterbury, 1979).

7. Conundrums of Aswan High Dam

I.   **Seepage losses.** These losses were underestimated. For example, when the Old Aswan Dam was filled in 1902, the reservoir initially lost 120 percent of its capacity, declining over a 30-year period to about nine percent of capacity. This was caused by the losses and porous nature of the underlying soils and rock. It was assumed that the same would happen at the High Dam and assuming the live storage capacity to be 100 bcm, he estimated that for at least 20 years total losses due to seepage and evaporation would be 124 percent of reservoir capacity. This was expected to stabilize at around 17 percent per annum after 30 years when the substrate reached saturation point (Waterbury, 1979).

II. **Evaporative losses from the Aswan High Dam.** This happens when taking wind velocity into consideration with equal 40 percent of storage capacity or 4 bcm. It is relevant when the original calculation was that Egypt would gain an additional 7.5 bcm annually from the High Dam as agreed with Sudan. This meant that the gains were in fact much lower than originally anticipated (Waterbury, 1979).

III. **Changes in hydrostatic pressure.** This underground water table would change the overall water balance (Waterbury, 1979). What this means is that by building a dam that raises the water table above the prevailing level in geological areas that are characterized by fissures and permeable beds, one reverses the flow of groundwater. Under normal conditions, water flows from the ground to the river, but once a dam is built and the water level is increased, water now flows from the river into the ground, being channelled away in underground fissures and being lost to the overall water balance of the basin.

8. Impacts of Aswan High Dam

I. The dam has not provided the benefits it was designed to bring. In fact, Egypt's water needs are greater than what the High Dam can satisfy, so the idea of theEquatorial Lakes as a source of supply is again gaining credibility (Waterbury, 1979).

II. Evaporative losses at the dam as discussed earlier have resulted in a reduced water quality downstream, with a higher saline content. Water flowing into the dam has a salinityof 200 ppm, and when it leaves, it is 220 ppm. But because of return flows back intothe main Nile, salinity around Cairo is 300 ppm (Waterbury, 1979).

III. The quiet and serious technical debate over the merits and demerits of the dam were never allowed to take place, because the High Dam Covenant branded such studies as suspect and anti-Egyptian (Waterbury, 1979).

12.7. Upstream and Downstream Countries' Politics

Upstream Countries

Most of the upstream countries are members of the East African Community. They include Ethiopia, Kenya, Uganda, Tanzania, Burundi, Rwanda, South Sudan and DRC. However, Rwanda, Burundi and DRC are core members of Great Lakes Region. These countries have tributes of the River Nile, which flow to Sudan and Egypt. The politics of upstream countries is characterized by the followings:

1. Autocratic regime
2. Repression of the citizens
3. Violent and ethnic Conflict
4. Irredentism and secession tendencies
5. Traditional ownership of Nile Waters (1,727 billion cubic meters)
6. Extreme poverty and underdevelopment
7. Weak economies and poor growth

Figure 1: Schematization of River Nile in the Hydropolitics

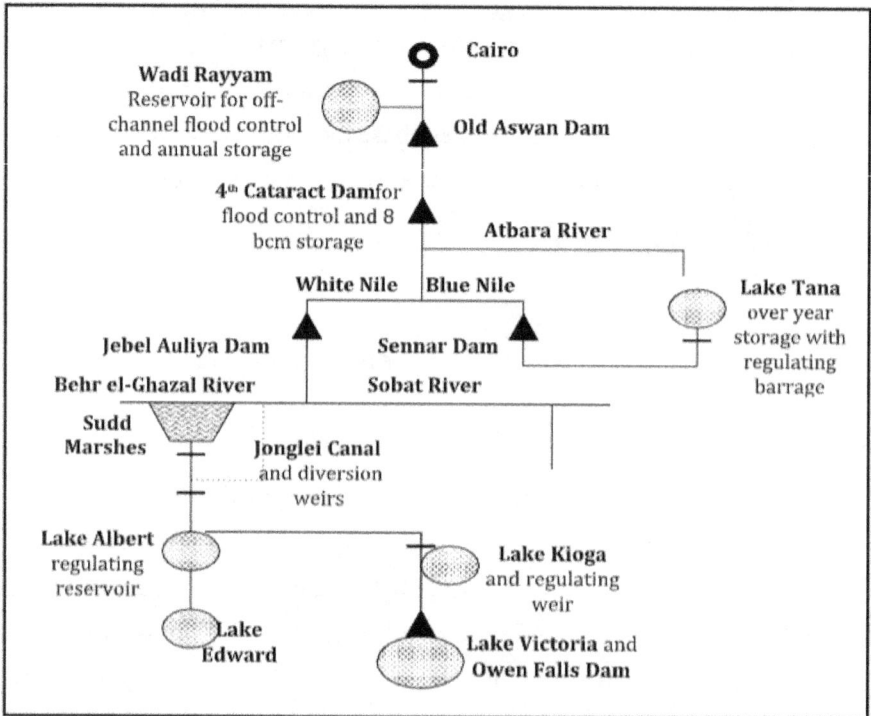

Source: Turton, 2000

Downstream Countries

Downstream countries are the recipients of Nile waters. They receive 73 billion cubic meters. Egypt receives 55 billion cubic meters while Sudan receives 18 billion cubic meters. The politics of these countries is characterized as follows:

1. Islamic laws
2. Autocratic regimes
3. Revolutionary tendencies
4. Strong economies. Egypt is the second growing economy in Africa after Nigeria and Sudan is the seventh
5. Colonial ownerships of Nile waters
6. Poverty and underdevelopment
7. Arid and semi-arid lands

12.8. Comparative Analysis of Ethiopia, Egypt and Sudan on Grand Ethiopian Renaissance Dam (GERD)

Egypt and Sudan are utterly dependent on the waters of the Nile River. Over the past century both of these desert countries have built several dams and reservoirs, hoping to limit the ravages of droughts and floods, which have so defined their histories. Now Ethiopia, one of eight upriver states and the source of most of the Nile waters has built the largest dam in Africa. Located on the Blue Nile twenty-five miles from the Ethiopian border with Sudan, the Grand Renaissance Dam begins a new chapter in the long, bellicose history of debate on the ownership of the Nile waters, and its effects for the entire region could be profound.In the fall of 2012 newspapers around the world reported on a *WikiLeaks* document, surreptitiously acquired from Stratfor, a Texas security company, revealing Egyptian and Sudanese plans to build an airstrip for bombing a dam in the Blue Nile River Gorge in Ethiopia. The Egyptian and Sudanese governments denied the reports.

Whether or not there were such plans in 2012, there is a long history of threats and conflicts in the Nile River Basin. Downstream Egypt and Sudan argue that they have historic rights to the water upon which they absolutely depend on and this is a matter of life and death. Indeed, in 1979 Egyptian President Anwar Sadat threatened war on violators of what he saw as his country's rights to Nile waters (Dellapenna, 1997). Upstream countries such as Ethiopia, Kenya, Uganda, Rwanda, Burundi, and Tanzania argue that they too need the water that originates on their lands and they can never compromise their positions.

Since the twelfth century C.E. Christian Ethiopian kings have warned of the Muslim Egyptian Sultans of power to divert waters of the Nile, often in response to religious conflicts. But these were hypothetical threats. Today, however, Ethiopia is completing the Grand Renaissance Dam and, with it, Ethiopia will physically control the Blue Nile Gorge—the primary source of most of the Nile waters.

Ethiopia, Egypt, and the Historical Struggle for the Nile's Waters
Ethiopia and Egypt have had a long relationship of both harmony and discord, the latter the result of religious issues and access to Nile water, among other factors. Ethiopia's first well documented government was in Aksum, a city-state that controlled a large empire from the Ethiopian highlands across the Red Sea to Yemen. From 100 until 800 C.E. Aksumites participated in Mediterranean and Indian Ocean trade. The cultural relationship between Egypt and Ethiopia was institutionalized when the Aksumite King Ezana converted to Christianity in 330 C.E. For sixteen centuries (until 1959) the Egyptian bishop of the Ethiopian Orthodox Church was appointed by the Egyptian patriarch in Alexandria, often under the influence of the Egyptian government.

Ethiopians were profoundly influenced by the Middle East, even writing their state and geography into Bible stories. The source of the Blue Nile became the Gihon, one of the four rivers that flowed from the Garden of Eden. In the 14th century C.E. myth of national origins connected Ethiopia's rulers to the Old Testament. In this legend, the Queen of Sheba (*Mekedda*), journeyed north from Ethiopia to Jerusalem to meet King Solomon in 900 B.C.E. A romantic relationship produced a child, Menelik I, the first in Ethiopia's Solomonic Dynasty. When Menelik became an adult, despite his father's wish that he become the next King of Israel, he escaped to Ethiopia with the Ark of the Covenant - the cabinet which contained the tablets of the ten commandments given by God to Moses on Mount Sinai. Menelik stored the Ark on an island in Lake Tana into which the Gihon flows—before it was moved to Aksum, where many Ethiopians believe the Ark remains to this day. Another Ethiopian legend is that Mary and Jesus stayed a night on the same island (Tana Cherquos) during their flight from the Holy Land to Egypt.

The Muslim conquest of Egypt in 640 C.E. put Christian Ethiopia in a defensive position. Because the Ethiopian Orthodox Church remained subordinate to the Orthodox Church in Alexandria and Egypt had become a Muslim country, Ethiopians became suspicious and resentful of the control Egypt had on the appointment of their Christian bishop (*abun*). Muslim Egyptians also controlled Jerusalem and had the power to expel Ethiopian pilgrims to their holiest of cities.

So, Ethiopians began to claim power over Egypt through control of the Nile. During the crusades, the Ethiopian emperor Lalibela (1190-1225)—who built a new Jerusalem in Ethiopia, safe it from Muslim occupation in magnificent, underground rock-hewn churches—threatened retribution by diverting the Tekeze River from its pathway north into Sudan (where it becomes the Atbara and then joins the Nile). The first Egyptian to write about the potential for an Ethiopian diversion of the Nile was the 13th century Coptic scholar Jurjis al-Makin (d. 1273).

Stories about Ethiopia's power over the Nile inspired the 14th-century European legend of Prester John, a wealthy Christian Ethiopian priest-king. In 1510, the legend returned to Ethiopia with Portuguese explorer, Alfonso d' Albuquerque, who considered the possibility

of destroying Egypt by diverting the Nile to the Red Sea. In 1513 d'
Albuquerque even asked the Portuguese king for workers skilled in
digging tunnels. Nothing came of the plan (Carlson, 2016).

But conflict between Egypt and Ethiopia continued, often as
proxy wars between Christians and Muslims on Ethiopia's northern
or south-eastern borderlands. The 16th century invasion of Ethiopia
by Ahmad Gragn, the Muslim imam from the Adal Sultante, was seen
as an Egyptian invasion to spur up hydro-conflict. In the 19th-century
Egypt and Ethiopia fought over control of the Red Sea and upper
Nile Basin. The climax came in 1876 at the Battle of Gura in present
day Eritrea where the Ethiopians delivered a humiliating defeat to the
Egyptian army.

Colonial-Era Conflicts over the Nile River
The European partition of Africa in the 1880s added huge complexity
to this conflict. It is imperative to recall that Egypt was colonized by
England in 1882. Ethiopia defeated the Italians at the Battle of Adwa
in 1896 becoming the only African country to retain its independence
during the "scramble for Africa." But colonization created many new
states in the Nile Basin (Eritrea, Uganda, Rwanda, Burundi, Kenya,
and Tanzania) and set off new competition for resources and territory.
Egypt was prized for the Nile Delta, a region of unsurpassed agricultural productivity. After the completion of the Suez Canal in 1869,
Egypt was also offered access to the Red Sea and the Indian Ocean. For
the British control of Egypt meant more profitable trade with India,
its richest colony. For the French, the canal offered quicker access to
Indochina, its most lucrative colony.

In the late nineteenth century, since controlling Egypt was the key
to Asian wealth, and since Egypt depended on the Nile, controlling the
source of the Nile became a major colonial goal. The French-English
competition for control of the Nile Basin climaxed in 1898 at Fashoda,
Sudan.

The French conceived of the idea of building a dam on the White Nile, so as to undermine British influence further downriver and establish east-west control of the continent. They organized a stupendous pincer movement with one group of soldiers traveling from East Africa across Ethiopia and the other from West Africa across the Congo.

The British heard of the French expedition and having just captured Khartoum ordered a fleet of gun boats and steamers with soldiers under the leadership of General Horatio Herbert Kitchener upriver to Fashoda, the site of the proposed dam. With fewer than 200 men, the French were embarrassed. In 1899 the two colonial powers reached an agreement which designated to France the frontiers of the Congo River and to England the frontiers of the White Nile.

The Fashoda Incident revealed how little Europeans understood about the Nile River. Thinking that most of the Nile waters came from the equatorial lakes (Victoria, Albert, Kyoga, and Edward), the English spent enormous energy on plans to increase White Nile water flows. First called the Garstin Cut and later the Jonglei Canal, the British intended to create a channel that would maximize water transfer through the great swamp-where half of it evaporated (Mitchel, 2017).

One of the most expensive engineering projects in Africa, it was terminated in 1984 by the Sudan People's Liberation Army, because of the severe disruption it brought to the lives of the indigenous peoples in the Upper Nile region. If the 300-mile-long Jonglei Canal had been completed, it would have increased water flows by nearly 4 billion cubic meters into the White Nile. However, the environmental devastation would have been quite severe to the indigenous communities.

Negotiating the Nile: Treaties and Agreements over the Nile Waters

Treaty negotiations about Nile waters started during the colonial era as England tried to maximize agricultural productivity in the delta.

In 1902, the British secured from the Ethiopian Emperor Menelik II an agreement to consult with them on any Blue Nile water projects, especially on Lake Tana. As the controlling imperial power in East Africa, agreements with Kenya, Tanzania, Sudan and Uganda were *pro forma*, internal colonial matters. After achieving its independence in 1922, Egypt negotiated the Nile Waters Agreement of 1929 with the East African British colonies. This accord established Egypt's right to 48 billion cubic meters of water flow, all dry season waters, and veto-power over any upriver water management projects. Newly independent Sudan in 1956 was accorded rights to 4 billion cubic meters of water. The Ethiopian monarch was not consulted at least in part because no one understood how much Nile water actually came from Ethiopia.

The 1959 Nile Waters Agreement between Egypt and Sudan was completed before all the upstream states achieved independence: Tanzania (1961), Uganda (1962), Rwanda (1962), Burundi (1962) and Kenya (1963). The signatories of the 1959 Agreement allocated Egypt 55.5 billion cubic meters of water annually while Sudan was allowed 18.5 billion cubic meters. These 74 billion cubic meters represented 99 of the calculated average annual river flow.

The treaty also allowed for the construction of the Aswan High Dam (completed in 1971), the Roseires Dam (completed 1966 on the Blue Nile in Sudan), and the Khashm al-Girba Dam (completed in 1964 on the Atbara River in Sudan). The treaty so negatively affected the upstream states that it provided the inspiration for the Nyerere Doctrine, named after independent Tanzania's first president, which asserted that former colonies had no obligation to abide by treaties signed for them by Great Britain.

Emperor Haile Selassie was offended by President Nasser's exclusion of Ethiopia in the Nile Waters Agreement and in planning for building the Aswan Dam. He negotiated the 1959 divorce of the Ethiopian Orthodox Church from the Orthodox Church in Alexandria, ending 1600 years of institutional relationship. He also began planning for several dams on the Blue Nile and its tributaries, contributing $10 million dollars from the Ethiopian treasury towards a study by the US Department of Reclamation resulting in a seventeen-volume report completed in 1964 and titled *Land and Water Resources of the Blue Nile Basin: Ethiopia*.

Nasser responded by encouraging Muslims in Eritrea (reunified with Ethiopia after World War II) to secede from Ethiopia. He also encouraged Muslim Somalis to fight for the liberation of Ethiopia's Ogaden region. Ethiopia won the war with Somalia in 1977-78 and retained the Ogaden. However, it is thirty-year war with Eritrea, an Egyptian ally, came at a tremendous cost. Haile Selassie was overthrown in 1974, and in 1993 Eritrea won independence and Ethiopia became a landlocked country - although it still possessed the headwaters of the Blue Nile. In the middle of the 1980s, rains failed in the Ethiopian highlands, causing a serious water crisis upriver and downriver. One million Ethiopians died as a result of drought and famine - made worse by civil war with Eritrea. Egypt averted disaster but Aswan's turbines were nearly shutdown, creating an electric power crisis; and crops failed in the delta, bringing the real prospect of famine.

As a result, Egyptians came to understand that their great Aswan Dam had not solved their historic dependency on upriver Nile water. In 1987, after years of hostile rhetoric, the Egyptian President Hosni Mubarak and Ethiopian President Haile Mariam Mengistu replaced the language of threat and confrontation with words of conciliation and cooperation. Then in the 1990s, the Ethiopian rains returned, and, remarkably, Hosni Mubarak redoubled efforts begun during the Sadat administration to build the Toshka Canal, one of the world's most expensive and ambitious irrigation projects. This plan would take 10 percent of the waters in Lake Nasser to irrigate Egypt's sandy Western Desert, increasing Egypt's need for Nile water even if they maintained their 1959 treaty share of 55 billion cubic meters.

In anger and disbelief, Ethiopian Prime Minister Meles Zenawi protested: "While Egypt is taking the Nile water to transform the

Sahara Desert into something green, we in Ethiopia—who are the source of eight-five percent of that water—are denied the possibility of using it to feed ourselves" (Ethiopia Today News, 2011).

Prime Minister Meles Zenawi then began plans for the Grand Renaissance Dam. International water law has not resolved differences about ownership of Nile Waters. The Helsinki Agreement of 1966 proposed the idea of "equitable shares" - and the idea was taken up again in 1997 by the United Nations Convention on the Law of Non-Navigational Uses of International Watercourses. A proposal for "equitable shares" was again put forward in the 1999 Nile Basin Initiative, which included all the affected countries. Unfortunately, the initiative did not resolve the conflict between Egypt and Sudan's claims of historic rights and the upper river states' claims for equitable shares.

In 2010, six upstream countries (Ethiopia, Kenya, Uganda, Rwanda, Burundi, and Tanzania) signed a Cooperative Framework Agreement seeking more water shares as discussed in the previously in this book. Egypt and Sudan rejected the agreement because it challenged their historic water rights.

The Grand Ethiopian Renaissance Dam (GERD) and Potential Hydro-Conflicts

The Grand Ethiopian Renaissance Dam (GERD, formerly known as the Millennium Dam and sometimes referred to as Hidase Dam, is a gravity dam on the Blue Nile River in Ethiopia that has been under construction since 2011. It is in the Benishangul-Gumuz Region of Ethiopia, about 15 km east of the border with Sudan. At 6,450 MW, the dam will be the largest hydroelectric power plant in Africa when completed, as well as the 7th largest in the world. As of August 2021, the work stood at 70% completion. Once completed, the reservoir will take from 5 to 15 years to fill with water (Tadese, 2017). On 31 March 2011, a day after the project was made public, a US$4.8 billion contract was awarded without competitive bidding to an Italian Salini

Costruttori and the dam's foundation stone was laid on 2 April 2011 by then Prime Minister Meles Zenawi (Rogers and Crow-Miller, 2017). The biggest of Ethiopia's water projects, the Grand Renaissance Dam, will have a reservoir holding 67 billion cubic meters of water - twice the water held in Lake Tana, Ethiopia's largest lake - and is expected to generate 6,450 megawatts of electricity (Tefaye, 2017).

The state-owned Ethiopian Electric Power Corporation optimistically reports that the Ethiopian Grand Renaissance Dam (GERD) was to be completed in 2015 at total cost of US$ 6.4 billion (Ibid). However, the major obstacle to completion is financing. The World Bank, the European Investment Bank, the Chinese Import-Export Bank, and the African Development Bank provided financing for some of the other dams; but concerns about the environmental and political impact of this latest dam have discouraged lenders. The International Monetary Fund suggested that Ethiopia put the dam on a slow track, arguing that the project will absorb ten percent of Ethiopia's Gross Domestic Product, thus displacing other necessary infrastructure development (Tadese, 2020).

Nevertheless, the Ethiopian government insists that it will stick with its schedule and finance the project domestically through government bonds. It probably will secure more help from China, a loyal ally and the world's major developer of hydroelectric power. The Ethiopians argue that the Grand Renaissance Dam could be good for everyone. They contend that storing water in the deep Blue Nile Gorge would reduce evaporation, increasing water flows downstream. As it is said, the government asked all the Ethiopians civil servants to contribute ten percent of their salaries to complete the construction of the dam. Most of the patriotic Ethiopians contributed. The first phase of filling begun in July 2020. The second phase of filling was completed on 19th July 2021. The third phase of filling was completed on 12th August 2022.

The Ethiopians also argue that the new dam will be a source of hydroelectric power for the entire region and will manage flood control at a critical juncture where the Nile Gorge descends from the Ethiopian highlands to the Sahel, thus reducing the risk of flooding and siltation, extending the life of the dams below stream. Egypt and Sudan are understandably concerned about Ethiopia's power over Nile waters. What happens while the reservoir behind the Grand Renaissance Dam is filling up, when water flow may be reduced twenty-five percent for three years or more? After the reservoir is filled what will happen when rains fail in the Ethiopian highlands? Who will get the water first?

The potential impacts of the dam have been the source of severe regional controversy and hydro-conflicts. The Government of Egypt, a country which relies heavily on the waters of the Nile, has demanded that Ethiopia cease construction on the dam as a precondition to negotiations, sought regional support for its position, and some political leaders have discussed methods to sabotage it. Egypt has planned a diplomatic initiative to undermine support for the dam in the region as well as in other countries supporting the project such as China and Italy (Mekonen et al., 2014). However, other nations in the Nile Basin Initiative have expressed support for the dam, including Sudan, the only other nation downstream of the Blue Nile, which has accused Egypt of inflaming the situation (Hassen, 2014: 16). Ethiopia denies that the dam will have a negative impact on downstream water flows and contends that the dam will in fact increase water flows to Egypt by reducing evaporation on Lake Nasser (Garrick, 2016). It has accused Egypt of being unreasonable; Egypt is demanding to increase its share of the Nile's water flow from 66 to 90 percent (Mehari, 2017). In the context of a difficult history, violence is a possibility, but good solutions for all can be achieved through diplomacy and leadership. On 20 February 2022, the dam produced electricity for the first time, delivering it to the grid at a rate of 375 MW. A second 375 MW turbine was commissioned in August 2022.

Ethiopia and the Lessons of Dam Building

One lesson from the last century of mega-dam building is that upstream countries have the most power when negotiating water rights. The first of the mega-dams, the Hoover Dam on the Colorado River in the United States, cost Mexico water. The Ataturk Dam in Turkey has had a devastating impact on downriver Syria and Iraq. China and Tibet control waters on multiple rivers flowing downstream to India, Pakistan, Myanmar, Bangladesh and Vietnam.

Another lesson is that mega-dams have enormous and unanticipated environmental impacts. The Aswan High Dam has disrupted the ecosystems of the river, the delta, and the Mediterranean with the results of reduced agricultural productivity and fish stocks. It also caused a series of seismic events due to the extreme weight of the water in Lake Nasser, one of the world's largest reservoirs. Although late to mega-dam building, Ethiopia is now making up for lost time. One of the tallest dams in the world was completed in 2009 on the Tekeze River in northern Ethiopia. Three major dams on the Omo and Gibe Rivers in southern Ethiopia are either completed or nearly so.

Ethiopians hope these water projects - which extend to 2035 with other Nile tributaries and river systems - will lift their country out of poverty. Similar large dams have produced economic miracles in the United States, Canada, China, Turkey, India, Brazil, and, of course, Egypt. Ethiopia's options for economic development are limited. With nearly 90 million people, it is the most populous landlocked country in the world. It is also one of the world's poorest countries—180 on the list of 190 countries in the United Nations Human Development Index for 2022. Sudan was 173 and Egypt was 121. This index rates countries based on life expectancy, education, and income, among other criteria. Part of Ethiopia's challenge is that 85 percent of the workforce is in agricultural commodities that bring low profits. Ethiopia is already leasing land in its southern regions to Saudi Arabia, India, and China for large irrigated water projects—despite severe land shortages in its northern region because it does not have the funds to develop this land on its own.

If Ethiopia cannot use its electricity generated from GERD for power and irrigation for all Ethiopians, how will it survive? If it continues and completes GERD project without bringing Egypt on board, how will Egypt response finally and what will the consequences for this response for Greater Horn and Middle East peace and stability? These are the pertinent questions to ponder on moving forward!

12.9. The Genesis and Impacts of Jonglei Canal Project

The Jonglei Canal project was proposed in 1904 by a British Civil Engineer, Sir William Garstin during the Anglo-Egyptian rule in Sudan. In 1946, the government of Egypt conducted Engineering Procurement Construction (EPC) study and plans took shape between 1954 and 1959 during the period of decolonization which included Sudanese independence in 1956. The purpose of the canal was to minimize evaporations in the Sudd Wetlands where over 50 percent of freshwater spread out into the vast and absorptive low topographical landscapes, preventing faster discharge downstream (Howell et al, 2010). If completed, the project would have covered a length of 350 km, a width of 54 meters, a depth of 4.5 meters, and a water carrying capacity of 25 million cubic meters per day with discharge of 4.8 billion cubic meters annually downstream to Sudan and Egypt (Mohammed, 2001).

The French engineering firm, Compagnie Des Constructions Internationales (CCI) was contracted by Sudan's Government in Khartoum to commence the digging of Jonglei Canal in 1978. When the Southerners heard about the construction of the canal, they demonstrated against it across big cities, Juba, Wau and Malakal. While the demonstrations were large and chaotic, the Juba demonstration was the largest and most chaotic in scale as it involved students in primary and secondary schools. The leader of the demonstration,

Figure 2: Map of Grand Ethiopian Renaissance Dam (GERD)

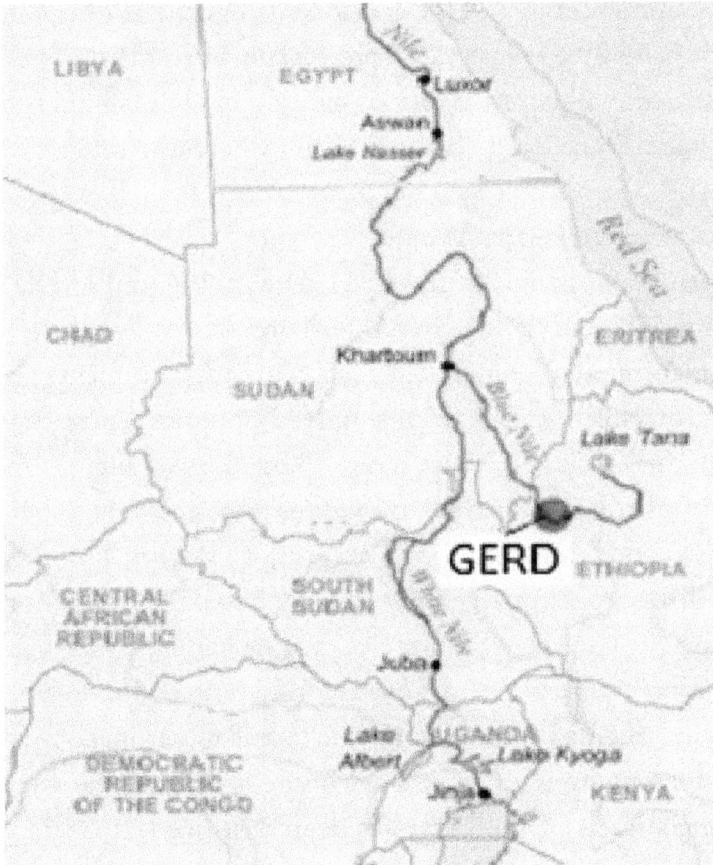

Source: Google Maps

Al-Zinc and three students were killed. Several politicians from the South were arrested. It has to be recalled that Chapter 5, article 14 (a) of the SPLM / A Manifesto of 31st July 1983 spelled out the construction of the Jonglei Canal and the involvement of Egyptians as the cause of massive unrest in the Southern Sudan.

The commencement of the civil in Sudan by the SPLM / A in 1983 led to the halt of the Jonglei Canal project construction in 1984. A piece of construction equipment (bucket wheel) was left behind between Twi East and Duk County in Jonglei state where its remains .

Impacts of Jonglei Canal Project

1. **Deaths**. Four people were killed led by Al-Zinc and several other politicians were arrested in the 1978 unrest.
2. **Displacement of people.** The canal caused displacement of people from the northern Twi to Duk to Ayod Counties. Those displaced from those villages did not return to the original site.
3. **Disruption of seasonal movement of animals**. The canal construction disrupted the movement of livestock and wildlife.
4. **Conflicts over grazing lands**. It has led to conflicts over grazing areas. The Nuer of Ayod and Dinka of Duk fought grazing land as the canal took a large tract of land from both communities.
5. **Environmental degradation.** Due to spillages from construction equipment, much of the environment around the construction channels of the canal has been destroyed. It is still pretty clear today as no vegetation has re-grown at the channel of the canals. This environmental pollution was perpetuated by the fact that the governments of Egypt and Sudan did not carry out an Environmental Social Impact Assessment (ESIA).
6. **Deep-Seated Mistrust.** Due to the way the canal was conceived, there is a deep-seated mistrust between the South Sudanese government and the Egyptian government. While the leaders of the government of South Sudan might have their personal interests

Figure 3: Pictorial of the Jonglei Canal in February-1984

Source: Google Maps

in the digging of the Jonglei Canal, South Sudanese citizens vehemently opposed it as they continued to mistrust Egypt.

12.10. The Role of South Sudan
in Nile Basin Countries' Politics

South Sudan plays a critical role in the balance of power between upstream and downstream countries. If South Sudan accedes to signing the Cooperation Framework Agreement (CFA), power will shift to the upstream countries; this will force Egypt and Sudan to renounce the 1959 treaty and accept cooperation on the basis of the CFA. However, if it doesn't, the upstream countries may decide to act unilaterally to the detriment of the lower riparian states. In this case, with a new regime in power, Nile riparian states may renegotiate an agreement that includes the needs of all Nile Basin Countries (NBI).

Therefore, South Sudan as a middle stream state has a responsibility to bring all Nile riparian states on table so that they can negotiate a lasting solution to the river Nile basin conflicts besides negotiating a lasting peace. South Sudan plays a big role at the heart of the Nile Basin Hydropolitics because 90% of its surface area falls under the Nile Basin. In addition, most rivers that feed the Nile have confluence in South Sudan. The Nile River is therefore not only critical to South Sudan's survival but also exposes South Sudan to conflicts not only with Sudan but also with other regional actors for instance, Egypt (Ufulle, 2011).

The use of the Nile River waters has led to an increase in the regional competition for water. All Nile basin countries are experiencing population growth at high rates (Tadesse, 2012). Gabriel Sultana (2019) argues that population increase would bring about the desire to explore water resources within their borders (Sultana, 2019). At the same time, Nile riparian states continue to depend on this river. Reports by the United Nations confirm that the Nile waters have been on the decrease over the past hundred years. In this case, South Sudan's demand for water is bound to increase rapidly in the coming years, thereby reducing Nile waters by a bigger percentage.

The allocation of water and establishment of hydro-infrastructure is central to economic, ecological and demographic development. South Sudan depends on oil revenues for 80% of its state budget; it also has great potential for Agriculture. It also has the potential for agricultural production. Building hydro-infrastructure could help generate electricity and divert water for irrigation. There has been a historic rivalry between North and South Sudan. South Sudan would face the greatest challenge of balancing cooperation with its own unilateral objectives, which its people sorely need. Governments of both countries are aware of the potential of the challenge of securing water, so they guard their own, while constantly looking for more to exploit; this fear leads countries to act unilaterally (Waterbury, 1979).

Option for South Sudan in Nile Basin Hydropolitics
As a middle upstream state, South Sudan is bound to take the following options: the first option is to maintain the status quo. South Sudan still benefits from the 1959 treaty agreement in that it is entitled to its annual flow of the Nile as per the agreement. Additionally, it is unclear under the post-referendum issues what share of water both South Sudan and Sudan are entitled to as they signed the treaty as one country in 1959.

The second option is to cooperate under the Nile Basin Initiative. Under this framework, all riparian states will benefit from equitable water distribution. It will also cement good relations.

Its last option is to pursue independent development projects. South Sudan is one of the least developed countries in the region; it is just getting on its feet. It has poor infrastructure; it has not developed major water resources and still experiences issues with sanitation. This option is detrimental to South Sudan because it still depends on Sudan for many things and if the country sets up such projects, they will take a very long time to be established.

Additionally, the entry of South Sudan as a middle-stream country is bound to change the balance of power in the Nile Hydropolitics significantly. Since its independence, South Sudan was expected to sign the CFA but it has not. This is because it still benefits from the 1959 Nile Agreement. Similarly, Eritrea remains an observer state since it is not located along the Nile or its tributaries, so not eligible to sign. With the CFA in place, the Nile riparian states may come together to establish another treaty that would ensure equitable use and distribution of the Nile waters and resources. If the CFA doesn't go through, downstream countries will continue to have a monopoly over the Nile. Therefore, South Sudan remains a key determinant in the shift of power in the Nile hydro-politics. The alliances that South Sudan is likely to form will most definitely border on its national interests (Ayebare, 2010).

The Ministry of Water Resources and Irrigation should scale up itself to magnify the importance of water, particularly, the Nile River, to South Sudanese and its Government. There is a need for South Sudan parliament to urgently enact Nile River Management Act to regulate management of Nile resources domestically and with its neighbours.

12.11. The Role of China in Nile Basin Politics

The growing intensification of economic, political and social ties between China and Africa in the last 20 years is often told as a story of copper, petrodollars, emerging China towns and bilateral visits by heads of state. But perhaps the most significant way in which Chinese actors are contributing to an evolving African political-economic landscape is very seldom discussed: an unprecedented wave of hydro-infrastructure construction is taking place. Beijing is a key partner for the construction of big dams, the expansion of irrigation systems and the building of transportation canals. This is recalibrating the domestic political economies of major African states and altering how they relate to each other. In the movie on how China met Africa, the desire for China relations with Africa is deeply rooted in socio-economic development and not politics per se.

Toppling Egypt's Hydro-Hegemony

Nowhere has China's returned to Africa been more consequential from a geopolitical water angle than in the Nile Basin, which covers eleven African states. For decades, the geopolitics of the Nile have been violent yet predictable. Despite being downstream, Egypt has for generations been the "hydro-hegemon": the country with the best economy; the largest population; the strongest military forces; the most international prestige; and the closest partnerships with global superpowers.

Cairo invaded Sudan and Ethiopia in the nineteenth century and intervened heavily in Sudanese politics throughout the twentieth century, whilst also standing accused of interference in Uganda and Ethiopia. The reason was simple: given their profound dependence on Nile water (97 percent of domestic consumption comes from the river), Egyptian elites developed a mindset that sought to maximize their control over water used throughout the basin (Chamgson, 2012).

Close relations with a succession of major powers-the UK (until the 1950s), the Soviet Union (until the mid-1970s) and the US ever since provided the political and financial backing to entrench Cairo's pre-eminent position in the basin through political-legal treaties, behind the scenes influence and actual construction of infrastructure for power generation, storage and irrigation. The record-breaking Aswan Dam was built after the 1959 Nile Waters Agreement reserved the bulk of the river's flow for Egypt. Egypt's pre-eminence was disliked in the Nile Basin, but chronic domestic crises in Ethiopia, Uganda and Sudan meant that countries further upstream could not do much about Cairo's hydro-hegemony. It was inconceivable that the international financial institutions would ever fund any major hydro-infrastructure projects upstream without Egypt's explicit permission, particularly given the close alliance between Washington and Cairo.

Moreover, as dams were no longer considered very useful in the strategies of development economists (they came to be associated with mass displacement, corruption and environmental damage) there was even less of an incentive for Addis Ababa, Khartoum or Kampala to invest in such costly projects, which were only feasible with massive external support. This began to change in the 1990s when several forces internal to the region collided with China's intensified role in Africa with massive funding for dams including GERD.

China Revives Old Ambitions

China's impact on the Nile Basin has been hugely consequential in two ways. The availability of Chinese technical skills, political support and capital has given African countries options that simply did not exist prior to the 1990s. While the World Bank had become reluctant to fund major hydro-infrastructure in the developing world, Chinese companies and banks, sensing profitable business opportunities, were very eager to help Sudan and Ethiopia harness their water resources and have since become major partners in the two most ambitious dam programmes in Africa.

Sino hydro, the world's leading dam builder, has been central to the construction of the Merowe dam and the heightening of the Roseires dam in Sudan; with the also state-owned China International Water and Electricity Corporation closely involved in these multibillion dollar projects as well. China has provided loans worth more than US$1 billion for Merowe and for Uganda's biggest hydro-infrastructure project, the Karuma dam construction of which is about to begin. Chinese public funds and enterprises have also been crucial to Ethiopia's dam-building. The Industrial and Commercial Bank of China is providing essential loans for the controversial Gilgel Gibe III dam after the World Bank, African Development Bank and European Investment Bank withdrew, citing ecological and social concerns. China is funding 30 percent of GERD through loan via Chinese Exim Bank.

Dams as "Soft Power"

But there has also been a second, more subtle form of influence exerted by Beijing. Big dams and hydro-engineering were crucial ingredients in China's own domestic transformation. The prominent role played by mega-infrastructure projects in Chinese industrialization has not gone unnoticed and is a form of soft power: as African countries have become disillusioned with "good governance" conditionality by traditional donors, and as the West's fortunes have declined with the Great Recession, alternative models of development and political order.

While the exact details of China's economic miracle remain relatively poorly understood in the Nile Basin, several regimes (which several of the Western academics and my self-termed "Africa illiberal state-builders" have embraced a vision of entrenching political hegemony in their respective countries not dissimilar to that of the Chinese Communist Party.

The combination of political authoritarianism with strategic control of key sectors in the economy is seen as essential to the long-term survival of the ruling party; there is a consensus among elites that jobs need to be created and services provided to key constituencies so that significant portions of the population (though not necessarily a majority) consider continuing rule and economic stability provided by the dominant party in their interest. Big infrastructure projects are an important element in this long-term economic strategy

The grand strategy of Africa's most famous illiberal state-builder, the late Ethiopian Prime Minister Meles Zenawi, is a good illustration of Chinese and Russian influence. Ethiopia's ruling coalition has built a deep relationship with its counterparts in Beijing and has attempted to draw important lessons from the Chinese experience, in agricultural reform and political control as well as in instrumentalizing the financial sector and crucially, developing hydro-infrastructure.

Zenawi designed Ethiopia's dam (GERD) programme as a nation-building project – tying peripheral regions to the political center - and turned it into the central axis of Ethiopian foreign policy, to acquire greater autonomy from the outside world and to link with Ethiopia's neighbors through energy flows. The programme was ironically a result of the erosion of the West's dominance, despite the World Bank's role in co-writing much of the technical details of the planned hydro-infrastructure. Ethiopia's ambitions are decades old, but were politically and financially unachievable until recently. China's huge new role in the Nile Basin has made all the difference in Ethiopia, Sudan and elsewhere.

Discontent at the Grassroots

The story of China's most underestimated export, however, is not all rosy. While enthusiasm for dam-building is widespread among Nile Basin governments, large segments of the Ethiopian, Ugandan and Sudanese populations are deeply skeptical about these plans. The Merowe dam and the enlarged Roseries dam displaced more than one hundred thousand people, many of whom already had antagonistic relations with the Sudanese regime and who blamed China for working with a violent, corrupt and exclusionary elite that does not provide adequate compensation or in the resettlement for the problems that have continued to-surface. Similar anger - including mass arrests and deadly protests - erupted in Southern Ethiopia over the Gibe dams, which threaten to ruin the livelihoods of tens of thousands of local communities, who will have to make way for capital-intensive sugar production, facilitated by irrigation waters released by the new hydro-infrastructure. If Chinese soft power in the economic realm is to be sustainable, far greater support from local populations for these mega-projects that are remaking East Africa is needed. While Chinese companies cannot assume tasks that a sovereign government should be responsible for, the increasingly ugly fallout from hydro-development projects should encourage a reconsideration of how a more effective contribution can be made to sustainably develop Africa's water resources.

12.12. Role of West (Britain) in Nile Basin Politics

When the British took control of Egypt in 1882, they very soon realized that they had become rulers of a society that was totally dependent upon the Nile. So, they understood from the very beginning that the economic stability, economic development and political stability of Egypt depended on Nile control. They also understood that in order to improve their own position within Egypt, they had to prove to the people of Egypt that they were able to provide water to them. From quite early on, the British also decided in a way to transform Egypt into a cotton farm for the textile industry in England. They also understood that in the long run, it might be very useful for London to have control over the Nile upstream of Egypt. So, if the need would arise, then they would have a potential power against Egyptian nationalism. This is known as a quite complex relationship between the hydrology of the Nile, the emerging water crisis of Egypt in the 1880s/1890s, regional power relations and the British strategy. All of these combined to create what was called in the 1890s the British road to imperialism (Adama, 2012).

Talking about the Nile River

In the 1890s, there was a growing awareness in Egypt that there was a water crisis coming. The gap between the demand for water and supply of water increased. There emerged a kind of Nile discourse in Egypt. A lot of people were engaged in talking about how to secure more water for Egypt. So, in the 1890s, already people had started to talk about the need for doing something with the Nile upstream of Egypt, in Sudan, in what is today Uganda. So, when the British decided to conquer the Nile basin, that was very much in line with contemporary thought among people interested in Nile control. To control the Nile, the British did a lot of things during the 1890s. First, of course, they occupied what is today Uganda in 1894. They occupied the headwaters of the White Nile. Secondly, they occupied, together with Egypt and Sudan between 1896 and 1898 – during the so-called River War. So, by 1898, they managed to control the whole White Nile.

But what about the Blue Nile? We know of course that the Blue Nile provides most of the water of the Nile. But at that time, it was very difficult to control the Blue Nile because of all the silt of the river (Ahmed and Elsanabery, 2015). They did not have the technology to build a dam that was able to control the Blue Nile all year. So, when it comes to the Blue Nile they decided upon another strategy. They entered into an agreement with the then emperor of Ethiopia – Emperor Menelik II, an agreement where, according to the British, the Ethiopians promised not to take any water from the Blue Nile without the prior notification of the British in Cairo (Seltel, 2015). This was the 1902 agreement according to the British story of it. So, by 1902, Britain controlled Uganda, Sudan, and Egypt - the whole area around Lake Victoria. It also controlled Kenya. And they had an agreement with Ethiopia, which secured the Blue Nile waters for Egypt and the Sudan. So, by 1902, Britain was the ruler of the whole Nile basin.

Taking the Nile River 'In Hand'

In about 1890, the British made it very, very clear to the other European powers struggling to get control of territories in Africa, that the Nile basin should be a British sphere of interest. This was in a way acknowledged by the other European powers. By the beginning of the 20th century, the British had diplomatic agreements with their European rivals acknowledging that the Nile basin was indeed a British sphere of interest. These agreements did not guarantee British control of the Nile but they made it possible. Britain had in a way a green light for implementing their own Nile basin strategy, which of course developed during the 1890s and the first decade of the 20th century into a real comprehensive strategy for utilizing the Nile water in accordance with the interests of the British Empire. The British brought engineers and water planners from India to Egypt. These technicians were very experienced guys. They gave them a lot of funds and a lot of political freedom so they really could take the Nile in hand. That was in a way the slogan of the British: "We want to take the Nile River in hand" (Williamson, 1958). "We want to turn the gifts of nature into the benefit of humankind" (Sortori, 1999).

The British were the first to really conceive of the Nile as one hydrological unit and therefore as one planning unit. From the 1890s, they came up with a number of plans: The Aswan Dam, they had plans for, the dam on Lake Tana in Ethiopia, they had plans for building dams on Lake Victoria in Uganda and they had plans for building Jonglei Canal through the South of Sudan. Most of the plans that people have been working on during the whole of the 20th century were plans drawn up by the British at the beginning of the century.

The British had very, very ambitious plans for the Nile. Some of the people they met thought that they were following on the footsteps of the builders of the pyramids - but that their plans were much more important. The plans that some of these water engineers had - they wanted to tame the Nile. Not only the British water planners, but all the British politicians were very ambitious indeed when it came to controlling the Nile. They didn't succeed in everything of course.

But at the turn of the century, they were really at the forefront. They built the Aswan Dam, the biggest reservoir of its kind in the world at that time in Egypt. And they had attempted to build a canal across the then Southern Sudan on a scale that nobody else anywhere was thinking about at that same time. However, their plans did not succeed as the SPLA stopped the construction of the canal in 1984.

When the British first started to develop Nile control in Egypt, they tried to improve the existing irrigation system that they found when they came. But very soon, they started to change the system into what they called perennial - that is an all-year irrigation system produces harvest for three seasons a year. The British were so concerned with improving the system of all-year irrigation because what they needed all the time was more water during the summer. The more water during the summertime, the more cotton they could cultivate. They tried to turn the fertile deserts of Egypt into an area that produces cotton for export in order to both create political stability in Egypt and economic wealth for Egypt. The British thought that this strategy was in the interest of the British and in the interest of the Egyptian people.

Guardians of the Nile

During the first decades of the 20th century, the British regarded themselves as the guardians of the Nile water, as the rulers of the Nile basin, as that political force that finally made it possible to turn the gifts of the Nile to the benefit of the people and to the benefits of the British Empire of course. But slowly, perhaps mainly because of a stronger anti-British political movement in Egypt, which ended of course in the Egyptian revolution in 1919 and perhaps (there was) a sign that the cotton farm in Egypt might be going extinct. So, what they did was to give more and more emphasis to the development of Sudan so that they can acquire the cotton too. The British wanted to use Nile waters in the Sudan for two reasons. They thought it was possible to grow cotton in Sudan. In 1902, they had discovered that it was possible to build a huge - perhaps the world's biggest - cotton farm in the Gezira area, an area between the White Nile and the Blue Nile in the Sudan (Mahmoud, 2001). They had fantastically ambitious plans for the Gezira scheme that envisioned an area bigger than the whole Nile Delta in Egypt.

As explained earlier, the Great Britain wanted to turn this area into a cotton-producing region because there was still a need in Britain for cotton. They wanted to substitute this kind of cotton in case Egyptian cotton became difficult to access if political problems between Egypt and Britain emerged. From the very beginning, the British thought that Sudan geopolitically speaking, held the key to Egypt. Why? They said and further thought that the Nile was coming far from the South, crossing three climatic zones and thousands of different ethnic groups of people. It would be very difficult to control from a downstream state like Egypt. But they also thought that by doing more hydrological work in Sudan, then it would be possible to develop a Sudan which would be more independent from Egypt. Moreover, the Britain hoped to use Sudan, a newly independent from Egypt as a kind of leverage against Egyptian nationalism.

So, they had dual purpose for the Gezira scheme. It would increase cotton production in Sudan for the benefit of the British textile industry. While signing, to Egypt and also to the Sudanese people that "Egypt was not really in control of all the Nile, the Nile is running through Sudan" (Damala, 1999). Then this begs the question. Who had the power in Sudan? The British had the power in Sudan, which meant that Egypt had to realize they would not always do what they wanted to do to upstream countries, because in Sudan, the British and also the Sudanese had plans to use the Nile. The Gezira was a way to create a rift between Egypt and Sudan and also create a Sudan more independent from Egypt.

So, when it comes to the Nile, the British in the Nile basin, then it made us to talk about a kind of imperialism that was both built and did not build. In other areas of the Nile Basin, they did not do that much for the same reasons. They put much more emphasis on the development in northern Sudan and Egypt than they did on the then Southern Sudan or present-day Uganda and present-day Kenya. These regions were meant not to use Nile waters in the spirit of 1929 and 1959 Agreements. So, there were viewed as not having played the same crucial role in the whole British scrambling strategy. It might be plausible to argue that the way the British developed Nile control increased the regional inequalities in the Nile basin. At the same time, it is also very important to acknowledge that the British were the first to really approach the whole Nile basin as one planning unit and, in this sense, as one hydrological unit. Britain was an imperial power with imperial strategic concerns. They also played the deepest power politics in the Nile basin.

CHAPTER THIRTEEN

13.1. Political Conundrums and the Changing World

The political conundrums refer to the challenges that have occurred in the world and that have changed the world order and contemporary world politics. These major political conundrums have shaped the empirical and normative understanding of comparative politics. While comparative politics like other branches of political science cannot be physically touched with hands and experimented in the laboratory like other natural or physical sciences, it has the ability to analyse and transform the world. Comparative politics then is great, analytical and coveted science. Next, we look at three major political conundrums that political science has been key in understanding:

13. 2. September, 11th 2001 Attack on the US

The 11th September 2001 attacks on the US were moments for global extremists and terrorists. Widely considered the most egregious act of international terrorism, the attacks on the US killed almost three thousand people (two thousand, nine hundred and seventy seven) victims plus the nineteen al-Qaeda terrorists), injured an estimated twenty-five thousand, and inspired attacks in Bali, Djerba, London, Madrid, and elsewhere (Frank, 2001). The horror of 9/11 galvanized the world to come together to try to defeat terrorism. To address the common threat, military forces, law enforcement authorities and intelligence services built common databases, exchanged personnel, conducted joint training and operations, shared intelligence, technology, expertise, and experience. The driving force behind the effort - the United States has continued to face a new set of daunting threats.

The consequences of the 9/11 can be explained as follows:

I. **Tight security surveillance**. Due to the occurrence of these acts of terrorisms, the US and its alliances commenced putting tight surveillance on all those who live in the US and at their allies' territories. Frequent security checks and searches were carried out and continued being carried out today. This tight security surveillance has changed politics, particularly, comparative politics, especially, the freedom to assembly and talking politics as people want.

II. **Stringent Border Control**. After the incident of 9/11, borders were stringently controlled. Not only in the US and Europe but across the whole world. This tight control has devastating impacts on politics. The conundrums of immigration control of people and particularly, Muslims, presented many challenges for scholars of comparative politics in transforming the nature and conduct of comparative politics.

III. **War on terror.** After September 2001, the US and its allies immediately invested more resources in the war against terror. The US government vowed to fight the al-Qaida networks and their sponsors. During this time, President George W. Bush (Jr.) took it as a personal matter to smoke out any terrorists in the world (Maranville, 2021). Enormous resources were earmarked to US-friendly states in Europe, South America, the Middle East, Asia and Africa and resulted in sustenance wars in Iraq, Somalia, Nigeria, Kenya and DR Congo. The arguments about these wars have rightly packaged them as "wars on terror."

IV. **American foreign policy turned into isolationism.** Due to the devastation caused by 9/11 on the US, the government of the US shifted its foreign policy to isolationism. This is whereby the US government decided to withdraw its foreign aid support to the developing world. This is the same time the US reduced its financial support to multilateral institutions such as United Nations, World Bank and IMF. This period ran from September 11th 2001 to January, 11th 2009 when President Barack Obama assumed the Office of the President of the United States of America. President Obama changed the isolationist policy to engagement policy known best as multilateralism. During this time, the US government realized the need to engage with the 'mad men' referring to an engagement with leaders of North Korea, Kuwait and Iran whom President Bush had declared as the *axis of evils* and feeble states run by 'mad men' (Sing, 2012).

V. **Change of world order.** With 9/11 attack, the world order was viewed as changing and indeed has changed. The United States as I argued earlier went into the isolationist mode. This gave an opportunity to other rival great powers such as Russia and China who decided to open up for globalization (Zeihan, 2022). Globalization was immediately embraced by Chinese President Xi Jing Ping and Russian President Vladimir Putin who opened up their migration, financial and service sectors for investments and competition. This became an impetus of the transformed world order. However, this short Russia and China dominant was quickly reversed by the US government who later embraced globalization and a competitive economy and politics.

13.3. Covid-19 Pandemic and its Consequences on Politics

Coronavirus also known as the Covid-19 pandemic is one of the conundrums that has transformed world governance and politics. While it is a health matter, it morphed into a political matter. It is a group of viruses that are found in animals such as bats and spread to human persons. Known as very infectious virus, the novel virus is caused by acute respiratory syndrome coronavirus 2 (SARS-CoV-2). It was first identified in Wuhan town of Hubei Province in China in November 2019. It quickly spread to Mainland China and then by March 2020 it had spread across the world. Its basic symptoms, include coughing, sneezing, high fever, sore throat and body aches amongst others. The death tolls as well as infections are in the millions. Families and workers have been affected and devastated. Although vaccines have been rolled out, they have not yet significantly and effectively halted the infections. While there are no more new infections at the time of writing this book, the Covid-19 pandemic is likely is to resurface in the world. The impact of this dreadful disease on jobs, the economy, the personal lives of people as well as politics globally is unprecedented (Alexis, 2021). Political scientists and industrial leaders of organizations have been overwhelmed and devastated in paying attention to numerous questions in regard to the management and leadership responses to Coronavirus disease. While these questions continued to be addressed by the leaders, the impacts of the Covid-19 pandemic on politics and particularly, comparative politics remained a conundrum that has changed the world through quick decisions. The Covid-19 conundrums are discussed below:

I. Enormous Deaths Toll

The deaths due to Covid-19 stand at 672,789,882 persons globally (Marasmus, 2022). While many scholars view this as social and economic consequence of the Covid-19 pandemic, it is a political consequence as well given the conundrum that led to the super spread of Covid-19 in the world. The Chinese and American governments continued to be blamed for poorly handling of the Covid-19 pandemic outbreak. Although the Chinese government argued that it informed the American government on time about the outbreak and fatality of the disease, the American government deeply blamed the Chinese government for holding back the vital information related to the Covid-19 pandemic. Although Covid-19 broke out in Wuhan town in Hubei province, central China, the death toll in China is less than in the US, India and France. This led to major political decisions in the US stringent ways of handling the Covid-19 pandemic leading to effective treatment as well as constant lockdowns. While it is correct to argue that majority of Americans were reckless and careless in regard to the prevention and management of Covid-19, the death tolls led to major political transformation (Zeihan, 2022).

II. Loss of Jobs

In 2020, about 115 million workers around the world lost their jobs or withdrew from the labor force due to Covid-19 pandemic (Marasmus, 2022). An estimated 30 million jobs were never created because of the disruption caused by the pandemic. It will take months or, in some sectors or locations, years for the labor force to recover. The International Labor Organization projects a shortfall of 23 million jobs even through 2023.

Peak unemployment rates in 2022 varied wildly, depending on the severity of the outbreak, the intensity and duration of containment measures, and the deployment of furlough schemes and government rescue packages. Midway through 2021, uncertainties remain. Governments, particularly in the advanced economies, are winding up support packages intended to defer or prevent bankruptcies and firings, with unforeseeable consequences. Elevated youth unemployment - which was bad enough in the short term - does long term damage to younger generations' ability to build wealth.

Optimistically, some experts hope the pandemic could spark a productivity boom, which has been absent in advanced economies for years. There's a stronger focus on the importance of creating high-quality jobs and ensuring that workers have the skills the employers need. And in developing markets, where informal labor is extremely prevalent, some governments are using the crisis to try to reform the labor system and bringing on informal workers out of the shadows.

III. Plummeting of Economies
China's Manufacturing Shock

According to a report by the China Enterprise Confederation (CEC) on 6th March 2021, over ninety percent of the three hundred large manufacturers surveyed had seen a revenue drop (Wenyang, 2022). In terms of consumption, compared to 2019, retail sales in January and February 2022 were down by 21.5% (Choi, 2023). Even though consumption started to be impacted by the pandemic in January, all retail sales apart from necessities were frozen as of February for almost the full month.

Fortunately, as China has been able to limit the spread of the virus, Chinese manufacturers have returned to full capacity. However, with the rest of the world going through various stages of lockdown, the country's economy is undergoing a second hit due to its overseas markets shutting down. Based on a paper from IMF economists, China will suffer from the cutback in global demand which accounts for 20 percent of the Chinese economy in 2023 (Wenyang, 2022).

According to Wang Pingfong (2023), one of China's top economists, we can expect a progressive recovery for China (Pingfong, 2023). However, based on a study from Cofetute, Chinese logistics and transportation consulting firm, 42 percent of citizens aim to reduce their spending as a precautionary measure for future unexpected events, whereas only 10 percent plan on shopping more after the outbreak (Pingfong, 2023). Although this could be worrying for businesses who rely on domestic custom, the expected recovery of China as a whole still brings hope and optimism to the rest of the world, where the situation is still evolving - especially in Europe and the United States of America.

United States Blues

In the United States for instance, with the quarantine measures continuously reducing economic activities, economists at Stanley Morgan (2020) have predicted a drop of 35 percent in consumption and a level of unemployment reaching approximately 13 percent in the second quarter of 2021 (Morgan, 2020). Indeed, the impact of the pandemic cannot be taken lightly, as it affects everyone directly or indirectly. The travel industry is among the sectors suffering the hardest hit, due to the travel restrictions implemented by governments worldwide.

With all the uncertainty lying behind Covid-19 pandemic, it is expected that the global market to be quite volatile, with no global growth this year. According to the Organization for Economic Cooperation and Development (OECD), it has been estimated that the global economy was going to decline by 2.1 percent by 2023 (Nanga, 2022).

Tom Rafferty, the main economist for China at the economist intelligence unit, suggests that, by 2023, global demand and supply should be back to normality. To achieve this result, policymakers have been obliged to review economic and business policies in order to mitigate the severity of the impact. However, the virus itself remains the last factor that will decide when each country can get back to a more 'regular' economic footing. Hopes have risen for the administration of the vaccines against Covid-19 pandemic. Descending voices argued against the effectiveness of the vaccines.

In March 2020, countries in the EU argued over decisions regarding financial government assistance to its citizens. Some states such as Spain and Italy argued for issuing debt bonds, while Germany opposed doing so. French President Emmanuel Macron has acknowledged the dangers the pandemic has caused for EU unity. As the United States' economy began to plummet, China accelerated its drive to replace America as the world's largest power. In Brazil, President Jair Bolsonaro has become more dedicated to the economy rather than the general public's health. Not to mention, President Bolsonaro's handling of the crisis has been blurred as his implications and scandals have taken over.

As explained above, the pandemic has led to global market failures and failed economies. However, resuscitation of these economies has begun and will continue till the global economies take up in the hope that no major catastrophes will occur again.

IV. Restricting Travel and Immigration

The Covid-19 pandemic led to restrictive immigration and travel across the world. From the US, Europe, Asia, Central, Africa and Oceanic, free travel was banned in the last three years. Right now, travels and immigration have been opened up only for those who have been vaccinated against the Covid-19 pandemic. While vaccination against Covid-19 has been globally rolled out, not all the people have been reached and not all the people have accepted to be vaccinated. There are those who argued from the religious point of view that vaccines are against God and thus should not be administered to the Christians, particularly, fundamentalists who believe in life after death (Chalade, 2022). This has now problematized the prevention of Covid-19 from the liberalists who advocate for vaccines and those conservatives who advocate against these vaccines. While having reached the cul-de-sac, the liberal advocates for vaccines have triumphed leading to the compulsory vaccinations for those who want to travel to other countries. Although travel has been opened up for people who are vaccinated to travels, there are a lot of health surveillances to ensure that any relapse of the Covid-19 pandemic is timely addressed. This health policy has transformed the political decisions in each of state in the world.

V. Conspiracy about the Genesis of Covid-19 and Politics Around it

There have been constants conspiracies against the origin of Covid-19 pandemic. While it is rightly known that the contagious disease originated from infected bats in Wuhan town markets at Hubei province, major conspiracists argue that it originated from a military laboratory in Wuhan manned by American soldiers. This conspiracy has been further advanced that the virus was manufactured by American doctor sponsored by CIA agents to destroy China and the world. These conspiracies are not only falsehood but also balderdash, bunkums and don't hold credible grain of evidence. If the US was responsible for the manufacturing of the virus, it would have not blamed China and WHO for failing to inform the American government on time. This led to Trump administration withdrawing US from the World Health Organization, after claiming that WHO was slow in updating members concerning scientific evidence and prevention against the Covid-19 pandemic. The United States' relationship with China has steadily become more fragile since the broke out of the novel virus in December 2019. With President Trump's then refusal to use the scientific name of Covid-19, and instead referring to it as the *"Chinese Virus"*, the mistrust between Beijing and Washington got deepened. In addition, escalations continued to rise when China expelled 13 American journalists in Wuhan accusing them of conspiring against Chinese state (Wales, 2021). China's Foreign Ministry announced in March 2020 that press credentials would not be renewed for American journalists representing The Wall Street Journal, the Washington Post, and the New York Times. The intensification of conflict between Washington and Beijing has left the bridge for business on a path to burning. The pandemic has made it more difficult for policymakers to focus their attention on other pressing matters. For example, strikes against US bases in Iraq happened and Congress did not get US troops out of the region. This crowding-out effect was supposed to be used to address the first two weeks of confusions in June 2021 when the government and media became tremendously focused on the Black Lives Matter protests, and abruptly forgot the pandemic that was resurging across the country.

CHAPTER FOURTEEN

14.1. Rethinking Comparative Politics

Comparative politics as mentioned in the introduction is one the deepest and most interesting branches of political science. Political science has remained as the master science amongst the social sciences. While political science has been akin to science of the government, it is a science of decision-making in a polity. With the ushering of comparative politics, the globe has been celebrating this holy and knowledge intensive sub-field of political science. However, a rethinking of this sub-field is imperative in the approach to research and teaching. This rethinking is important on the structural changes of comparative politics from qualitative methodologies to quantitative one. Qualitative comparative politics including theoretical and narration including argumentations. On the other hand, quantitative comparative politics include the use of data and the application of the systematic scientific survey tools such as STATA, SPSS and other statistical tools.

While many political scientists and preferably comparative political scientists are stuck with qualitative comparative politics, a new shift in comparative politics to quantitative methods is very necessary as given. The nature of comparative is very detailed and data-driven. Universities and institutions of higher learning who administer comparative politics as a sub-field need to fully move to quantitative comparative politics supported by dataset. While a lot of students and teachers view quantitative comparative politics as hard and mathematical in real sense of the words, they are basically assuming. Quantitative approaches are far much easier than qualitative approaches as the interpretation and application of knowledge are measured and easily retrieved. Because of the bazaar of evidence, comparative politics is being taken as a science and thus we are todays at the universities teaching masters of science in comparative politics referring to the same notion that comparative politics should be quantitative than qualitative.

While several caveats could be advanced as the use of dataset and the interpretation of the data limiting in most cases encouraging personal reflections and common sense, some of these caveats are not so strong and hence, comparative politics should continue to triumph as a great science and it should go anywhere as widely argued by the comparative politics scholars. Although comparative political scientists should move to a quantitative approach, this transition should be gradual enough so that those students and professors who have not been trained on methods should do so and fully transit to quantitative methods by 2033, allowing sufficient time to put resources together and train both students and professors in quantitative comparative politics. Since, its debut in political science, comparative politics has remained as a centre of inquiry into politics using comparative methods rather than a particular object of study. This makes it unique since all the other subfields are orientated around subjects or focuses and not specific subject or single focus of study.

REFERENCES

Abdalla, H. (1971). *The 1959 Nile Waters Agreement in Sudanese-Egyptian Relations.* Taylor & Francis.

Ackerman, B. (2013). *The Decline and Fall of the American Republic.* Belknap Press.

Adama, O. (2012). Urban Governance and Spatial Inequality in Service Delivery: A case Study of Solid Work Management in Abuja, Nigeria. Waste Management & Research. *The Journal for a Sustainable Circular Economy.* Vol 30 (9): 210-228

Adebayo, A. (1986). *Towards a Dynamic African Economy.* Taylor and France.

Ahmed, A and Elsanabery, M. (2015). Hydrological and Environmental Impacts of Local Ethiopian Renaissance Dam on the Nile River. *International Water Technology Journal.* Vol 5 (4): 101-121.

Aissa, H. (2012). *The Arab Spring: Causes, Consequences and Implications.* Arab Spring Newsletter.

Alexis, J. (2021). The Impact of Fear of Covid-19 on Job Stress. *Journal of American Psychological Association.* Vol 27 (1): 52-59.

Almond, G. (2007). *Comparative Politics Today: A World View.* Pearson Publishers.

Almond, G. (2017). *Structural Functional Approach.* UPSC Preparation.

Almond, G and Coleman, A. (1960). *Political Systems: Meaning, Functions and Types of Political Systems.* Puja Publishers.

Anderson, O. (1991). *Imagined Communities: Reflections on the Origin and Spread of Nationalism.* Verso Publishers.

Appadorai, P. (1968). The Importance of Cabinet Decision. *Journal of Governance.* Vol 2 (4): 95-115

Armstrong, J. (2017). *Nations Before Nationalism.* University of North Carolina Press.

Aristotle, A. (1888). *The Politics.* Athens Press.

Arthur, K. (1979). *Unequal Distribution of Economic Resources in Kenya.* Maranga Publishers.

Arguelles, L. (2009). *Proportional Representation in Non-Parliamentary System.* Good Books Publishers.

Asha, A. (2005). *Species in Europe: Biological Characteristics and Practical Guidelines for Sustainable Use.* Oxford University Press.

Ayebare, S. (2010). *A Political Storm Over the Nile.* International Peace Institute.

Barasa, K. (1993). *Deepening of Ethnic Politics in Kenya.* Palgrave.

Barry, A. (1999). *The Impact of Hutu Manifesto of 1957.* Kigali Publishers.

Bayart, F. (2009). *The State in Africa: Politics of Belly in Africa Polity.* Addison-Wesley Longman.

Bereketeab, R. (2012). *Self-Determination and Secession: A 21ˢᵗ Century Challenge to the Post-Colonial State in Africa.* Nordic African Institute. Uppsala-Sweden.

Bertalanffy, A. (1968). *General Systems Theory.* Oxford University Press

Blondel, J. (1969). *The Role of Legislatures in Institutional Strengthening.* Bloomberg Publishers.

Bok, N. (1996). *Structural Mobility and Economic Growth.* Macmillan.

Bonacich, E. (1973). *A Theory of Middleman Minorities.* American Sociological Review.

Bourdieu, P. (1990). *Structures, Habitus, Practices: Pierre, the Logic of Practices.* Polity Press.

Brehem, et al (2014). Genocide, Justice and Rwanda's Gacaca Courts. *Journal of Contemporary Criminal Justice.* Vol 30 (3): 333-352

Brown, S. (2004). Theorizing Kenya's Protracted Transition to Democracy. *Journal of Contemporary African Studies.* Vol 22 (3): 325-342

Brown, R. (1990). *Structural Functional Approach.* Palgrave.

Brubaker, R. (2006). *Ethnicity Without Groups.* Harvard University Press.

Brumberg, D. (2002). Transitions to Democracy. *Journal of Democracy.* Vol 1 (3): 113-133

Carothers, T. (2002). The End of the Transition Paradigm. *Journal of Democracy.* Vol 7 (3):110-132

Chalade, S. (2022). The Contests Against Covid-19 Vaccine. *Journal of Science.* Vol 5 (2): 112-122

Chamgson, I. (2012). *The Modern Political History of Egypt and River Nile.* Misri Publishers- Cairo

Chandra, K. (2007). *Why Ethnic Parties Succeed?* Cambridge University Press.

Chayes, S. (2016). *Thieves of State: Why Corruption Threatens Global Security.* Norton.

Choi, M. (2023). *Chinese Post-Covid-19 Economy Recovery.* Shanghai City Publishers.

Chol, J. (2021). *South Sudan State Formation: Failures, Shocks and Hopes. Africa* World Books Press.

Chol, J. (2014). Accommodating Deep Ethnic Differences: What was Done Right and What was Done Wrong? *Journal of Ethnic Studies.* Vol 1 (5): 121-146

Chol, J. (2012). Argument About Scientific Standards. *New Cues.* New York.

Clarke, A and Stone, B. (2011). *The Logic of Political Survival.* The MIT Press.

Churchill, W. (1948). *Democracy, the Worst Form of the Government. Royal* Printers.

Clinton, H. (2009). Foreign Policy Address at the Council on Foreign Policy Address at the Council on Foreign Relations. *Speech.* Washington, DC.

Coplan, D. (1971). *The Evolution of Social Science Theory.* Princeton University Press.

Collier, et al. (1993). Conceptual 'Stretching' Revisited: Adapting Categories in Comparative Analysis. *The American Political Science Review.* Vol 87 (4): 845-855

Collier, P and Levitsky, S. (1999). *Democracy with Objectives: Conceptual Innovation in Comparative Research.* World Politics.

Common, J. (2002). *The Concept of an Institution.* Basic Books.

Conner, W. (1994). *Ethno-nationalism: The Quest for Understanding.* Princeton University Press.

Dahl, R. (2009). Majoritarian Tranny in Politics. *Journal of Political Economy.* Vol. 2 (4): 121-146

Dahl, R. (1989). *Democracy and Its Critics.* Yale University Press.

Dallaire, R. (2009). *Shae Hands with the Devil: The Failure of Humanity in Rwanda.* Random House of Canada.

Damata, R. (1999). Is Egypt the Really Owner of River Nile? *African Union Briefs.* Addis Ababa.

Davies, M. (1996). *Democracy and Its Meaning.* Chicago university Press.

Decalo, S. (1998). The Process, Prospects and Constraints of Democratization in Africa. *Journal of African Affairs.* Vol 91 (362): 7-35

Dellapenna, J. (1997). *The Nile as a Legal and Political Structure.* Peking University.

De' Waal (2014). When Kleptocracy Becomes Insolvent: Brute Causes of the Civil War in South Sudan. *Journal African Affairs* 113 (452): 347-369

Diamond, L. (2003). *Developing Democracy: Towards Consolidation.* The Johns Hopkins University Press.

Diamond, L. (1966). Ethnic Configuration in Kenya. Palgrave.

Duman, Y. (2017). *Peacebuilding in a Conflict Setting: Peace and Reconciliation Committees in De Facto Rojava Autonomy in Syria.* Semantic Scholar.

Douglas, M and Wildavsky, A. (1983). *Risk and Culture: An Essay on the Selection of Technological Environmental Dangers*. Berkeley University of California Press.

Easton, D. (1953). *Political System Theory*. Oxford university Press.

Eberstadt, N. (1995). *The Tranny of Numbers. Measurement and Misrule*. The AEI Press.

Eshiwani, G. (1991). *The Roots of Ethnic Animosity*. East African Educational Publishers.

Ezbakha, F and Brehant, C. (2021). *Hydropolitics Remains as Politics*. Palgrave.

Fearon, D and Laitin, D. (1996). Explaining Inter-ethnic Cooperation. *American Political Science Review*. Vol 90 (4): 715-735.

Fleiner, S. (2008). *Function-Majoritarian or Consensual Democracy*. Princeton University.

Frank, W. (2011). *September 11th and the Aftermaths in World Politics*. New Yorker.

Freedom House *Report, 2022*.

Fukuyama, F. (1992). *The End of History and the Last Man*. Free Press.

Furia, P & Lucas, R. (2006). Determinants of Arab Public Opinion on Foreign Relations. *International Studies Quarterly*. Vol 50 (3): 585-605.

Gallagher, M and Hanson, J. (2013). *Authoritarian Survival, Resilience and the Electorate Theory*. Syracuse University Press.

Gamal, T. (2015). *Nile Water Agreement*. Water Management Institute. Cairo-Egypt.

Gardner, H. (2011). *Frames of Mind: The Theory of Multiple Intelligence*. Basic Books.

Garrick, D. (2016). The Hydropolitics of the Nile Revisited: Elites, Experts and Everyday Practices in Egypt and Sudan. *Global Environmental Politics*. Vol 16 (3): 151-156

Geddes, B. (1999). What Do We Know About Democratization After Twenty Years. *Annu. Rev. Polit. SCI*. Vol 1 (2): 115-144.

Geertz, C. (1963). *The Integrative Revolution: Primordial Sentiments and Civil Politics in the New States*. Macmillan

Godana, B. (1985). *Africa's Shared Water Resources: Legal and Institutional Aspects of the Nile, Niger and Senegal River Systems*. Francis Printer, Ltd. London.

Helmke, G. (2002). The Logic of Strategic Defection. *American Political Science Review*. Vol 96 (2): 291-311

Horowitz, D. (1985). *Ethnic Groups in Conflict*. University of California Press.

Howell, P et al (2010). *The Jonglei Canal: Impact and Opportunity*. Cambridge University Press.

Hutchinson, J. (2000). *Knowledge Calibration: What Politicians Know*. Palgrave.

Huntington, S. (1996). *The Clash of Civilizations and the Remaking of World Order*. Simon & Schuster Paperbacks.

Huntington, S. (1993). *The Third Wave: Democratization in the Late 20th Century*. University of Oklahoma Press.

Jensen, R. (1984). Historiography of American Political History. *Encyclopaedia of American Political History*. Vol. 1 (2): 1-25.

Jones, A. (2015). *The State of Burundi and the Conflict*. Bujumbura City Press.

Kalleberg, A. (1983). *The Concept of a Theory*. Oxford University Press.

Kasfir, N. (1976). *The Shrinking Political Arena: Participation and Ethnicity in African Politics. A case Study of Uganda*. University of California Press.

Khanfar, W. (2011). *Aljazeera and Democratization: The Rise of Arab Public*. Global Press.

Klare, M. (2002). *Resources Wars: The New Landscape of Global Conflict*. Henry Hott and Company.

Kliot, N. (2005). *Water Resources and Conflict in the Middle East*. Routledge.

Kissane, C. (2012). The Way Forward for Political Development in the World. *Journal of International Studies*. Vol 3 (4): 10-28

Knobelsdorf, V. (1999). *The Nile Water Agreements: Imposition and Impacts of Transboundary Legal System*. Yale University Press.

Kymlicka, W. (1995). Multicultural Citizenship: A liberal Theory of Minority Right. Oxford University Press.

Landman, T. (2008). *Issues and Methods in Comparative Politics*. Routledge.

Lerner, M. (1968). "Modernization. Social Aspects" in David L. Sills (ed.), *International Encyclopedia of the Social Sciences*. Vol. 10 (3): 386-411. New York: The Macmillan Company & the Free Press.

Lemarchand, R. (1996). *Burundi Ethnic Conflict and Genocide*. Cambridge University.

Lijphart, A. (2010). *Patterns of Democracy: Government Forms and Performance in Thirty-Six Countries*. Yale University.

Lijphart, A. (2009). *Consociational Democracy*. New Haven and London. Yale University Press.

Lincoln, A. (1865). *What is Democracy*. Washington University Press.

Linz, J and Stepan, A. (1996). Towards Consolidated Democracies. *Journal of Democracy*. Vol 7 (2): 126-146.

Lipset, S. (1955). *Democracy and Economic Development*. Washington DC.

Little, D. (2017). *Law, Religion and Human Rights*. Cambridge University Press.

Loewestern, J. (1965). *Importance of Institutions*. Zed Books.

Lonsdale, D. (1992). *Relationship Between Pastoralist and Agriculturalist Communities*. Luanda City Printers.

Lustick, et al (2004). *Crisis Early Warning and Decision Support. Contemporary Approaches and Thoughts on Future of Politics*. Macmillan.

Macridis, R. (2004). *Comparative Politics, Notes and Readings*. Yale University Press.

Marcel, M. (2011). The Gift Giving. *American Sociological Review*. Vol 29 (4): 105-125.

Mair, P and Rose. R. (2010). *Comparative Politics: Political Science, Empiricisms and Forms of Government*. Oxford University Press.

Mair, L. (1962). *Primitive Government*. Cambridge University Press.

Magstadt, T. and Schotten, P. (1999). Understanding Politics, Ideas, Institutions and Issues. *Journal of Comparative Governance.* Vol. 2 (30): 110-122.

Mahmoud, E. (2007). Environmental Scarcity, Hydropolitics and the Nile: Population Concentration, Water Scarcity and the Changing Domestic and Foreign Politics of the Sudan. *Published Thesis of Social Studies*, the Haque-Netherlands.

Mamdani, M. (2001). Beyond Settler and Native as Political Identities: Overcoming the Political Legacy of Colonialism. *Comparative Studies in Society and History.* Vol 3 (43): 651-664.

Mannheim, K. (1946). *Political Ideology.* Oxford University Press.

Maranville, A. (2021). *The 9/11 Terrorist Attacks: A Day that Changed America. Global Publishers.* Washington, DC.

Marasmus, A. (2022). Global Deaths Toll from Covid-19 Pandemic. *White House Briefs.* Washington DC.

Marter, G. (2001). *Comparative Political Science and Study of Patterns.* Harvard University Press.

McAdam et al. (2007). *Dynamics of Contentious Politics.* Centre of Social Change.

Mekonen, N et al. (2014). *Eastern Nile Basin Water System Simulation Using Hec-Ressim Model Part of the Water Resource Management Commons.* Water Development Institute.

Melvern, L. (2000). *A People Betrayed: The Role of the West in Rwanda's Genocide.* Zed Books.

Merton, R. (1981). *Theory of Functionalism.* Global Press.

Methari, T. (2017). *A Regional Power in the Making: Ethiopian Diplomacy in the Horn of Africa.* Ethiopian's Diplomacy in the Horn of Africa.

Migdal, J. (1988). *Strong Societies and Weak States.* Princeton University Press.

Mitchell, D. (2018). *Ethnic Corruption. Journal of Political Economy.* Vol 3 (4): 121-142.

Mitchell, J. (2017). The Epistemology of Emotional Experience. *Dialectical.* Vol 71 (5): 192-212

Model, J. (2009). *The Concept of Economy of Ethnicity.* Palgrave.

Moore, E. (1966). *Interval Analysis.* Prentice Hall. Englewood Cliff.

Mohammed, O. (2011). *Environmental and Socio-Economic Impact of the Jonglei Canal Project. Executive Organ for the Development Projects.* Jonglei Canal Area.

Molinga, P. (2008). Water, Politics and Development: Framing a Political Sociology of Water Resources Management. *Journal of Water Alternatives.* Vol 1 (1): 7-23

Morgan, S. (2020). *US Economy in Covid-19 Pandemic Times.* Washington DC.

Munick, B. (1996). *Quality Institutions and Democratization in Africa.* Palgrave.

Naimi, S. (2012). *Syria and Triangular Relationship.* Middle East Foreign Policy.

Nanga, B. (2022). Shocking Decline of the Global Economy in 2023. *Boston Briefs.* Boston City.

Nasr, J. (2000). Weak States and National Security Crisis. Palgrave.

Nathan, A. (2003). Authoritarian Resilience. *Journal of Democracy.* Vol 3 (14): 6-17.

Ndegwa, S. (1997). Citizenship and Ethnicity: An Examination of Two Transition Movements in Kenyan Politics. *American Political Science Review.* Vol 1 (91): 599-616.

Nnoli, O. (2007). *Ethnic Politics in Nigeria and the Consequences.* Basic Books.

Norris, C. (2005). *Investment in Human Development.* Basic Books.

Nwabueze, B. (2004). *Constitutional Democracy in Africa.* Ibadan- Spectrum Books- Nigeria.

Nyaba, P. (1997). *The Politics of Liberation in South Sudan.* Fountain Publishers.

Nyukuri, B. (1997). *The Impact of Past and Potential Ethnic Conflict on Kenyan's Stability and Development*. The USAID Conference on Conflict Resolution in the Greater Horn of Africa.

Obama, B. (2008). *What He Believes In: From His Own Works*. University of Chicago Press.

Obengo, J. (2016). Hydropolitics of the Nile: The Case of Ethiopia and Egypt. *African Security Review.* Vol 25 (1): 1-9

O'Donnell and Schmitter, P. (1986). *Transitions from Authoritarian Rule*. JHU Press.

Ogot, B. (1996). *Ethnicity, Nationalism and Democracy in Africa*. Institute of Research and Postgraduate Studies. Maseno University.

Pinaud, C. (2014). South Sudan: Civil War, Predation and the Making of a Military Aristocracy. *Journal African Affairs.* Vol 113 (451): 192-211

Pingfong, W. (2023). *Chinese Economy Recovery is Real*. Wuhan Publishers.

Plamenatz, J. (1970). *Ideology.* Oxford University Press.

Powell, B. (1988). *Comparative Politics Today: A world View*. Brown College Division,

Prezeworski, A. (2003). *Democracy and the Rule of Law.* Cambridge University Press.

Prezeworski, A. (2000). *Democracy and Development: Political Institutions and Well-Being in the World, 1950-1990.* Cambridge University Press.

Price, J. (2003). *The Composition of a Theory*. Macmillan Publishers.

Puddington, A and Roylance, F. (2021). *Dictators Differ from Democratically Elected Leaders in Facial Warmth*. Social Psychological and Personality Science.

Ray, L. (2004). *Comparative Governments*. Princeton University Press.

Ray, L. (2000). *Comparative Government and its Approaches*. Palgrave Macmillan.

Regier, T and Khalidi, M. (2009). The Arab Street: Tracking a Political Metaphor. *The Middle East Journal.* Vol 2 (4): 121-146.

Rogers, S and Crow-Miller (2017). The Politics of Water: A Review of

Hydropolitical Framework and their Application in China. *Wiley Interdisciplinary Reviews Water.* Vol 4 (6): 1239-1259

Rothschild, A. (1981). *Inter-ethnic Consociationalism.* Paris Paste Printers.

Rueschemeyer et al. (1992). Capitalism and Democracy: The Importance of Social Class in Historical Competitive Perspective. *Journal of Inter-American Studies and World Affairs.* Vol 34 (4): 225-244.

Schedler, A. (1998). What is Democratic Consolidation? *Journal of Democracy.* Vol 9 (2): 91-107.

Schimitter, P and Karl, T. (1991). What Democracy is and What Democracy is Not. *Journal of Democracy.* Vol 2 (3): 75-88.

Settel, A. (2015). *The Genesis of Nile River: Past, Present and Future.* Palgrave.

Sham, M. (2016). *Sectarianism and Its Discontents in the Study of Middle East.* Middle East Publishers.

Sortori, P. (1999). *The River Nile Historical Disputes. Journal of Modern African Studies.* Vol. 35 (4): 675-694.

Sievers, E. (2011). Theories on Territorial Sovereignty: A Reappraisal. *Journal of Sharia & Law.* Vol 41 (3): 118-129.

Singh, R. (2012). *Barack Obama's Post-American Foreign Policy: The Limits of Engagement.* Bloomsbury Academic.

Smith, A. (2009). *Ethno-Symbolism and Nationalism: A Cultural Approach.* Routledge.

Sodaro, M. (2007). *Comparative Politics: A Global Introduction.* McGraw-Hill.

Sodaro, M. (2001). *Comparative Politics:* A Global Introduction. McGraw-Hill.

Stearns, J. (2012). *Dancing in the Glory of Monsters: The Collapse of the Congo and the Great War of Africa.* Public Affairs.

Sultan, F. (2019). *Water Politics: Governance. Justice and the Right to Water.* Routledge.

Sussie, B. (1992). *Structural Functional Theory.* Harvard University Press.

Tanzi, V. (1998). *The Concept of Corruption and Its Effects.* Oxford University Press.

Tedla, N. (2013). *Analysis of Past Agreements on the Nile on View of the Law of Treaty and CFA.* Nile Publishers.

Tadese, J. (2020). *The Ground Ethiopian Renaissance Dam (GERD): Diplomatic War Between Ethiopia and Egypt. Power Relation Hegemony and Inequality.* Basic Books.

Tadasse, G. (2012). *Ethiopia Hydropower Development and Nile Basin Hydropolitics.* Aims Press.

Tesfaye, Z. (2017). *Hydropolitics and the Impacts on Ethiopian Government.* Addis Ababa University Press.

Tiemessen, A. (2005). *Competitive Identities in a Polity.* Princeton University Press.

Tilly, C. (2008). *Practice of Contentious Politics. Social Movement Studies.* Vol 7 (3): 225-246

Tocqueville, A. (1962). Comparative Political Analysis. *Journal of Comparative Politics.* Vol. 1 (2): 132-164

Turton, A. (2000). A Cryptic Hydropolitical History of the Nile for the Students of Hydropolitics. *African Water Issues Research Unit.* University of Pretoria.

Ufulle, G. (2011). *Water Security and Hydropolitics of the Nile Rivers: South Sudan's National Security in the 21ˢᵗ Century.* Research Gate.

United Nations Educational Scientific and Cultural Organization (UNESCO), *Report,* 2011.

Uvin, P. (1998). *Aiding Violence: The Development Enterprise in Rwanda.* Kumarian Press.

Vanhanen, T. (2012). National IQ: A Review of Education, Cognitive, Economic, Political and Demographic. *Intelligence Studies.* Vol 40 (2): 226-234

Vondeth, N. (2005). *Foundation of Comparative Politics.* Cambridge University Press.

Voros, J. (2006). Nesting Social-Analytical Perspectives: An Approach to Macro-Social Analysis. *Journal of Future Studies.* Vol 11 (1): 1-21

Wales, A. (2021). America and China Trade Virus Blames. *Journal for Political Economy.* Vol 2 (4): 101-132

Warner, W. (1949). *Social Class in America: A Manual of Procedure for the Measurement of Social Status Science Research Associates.* Wild Publishers.

Watts, H and Chattopadhyay, A. (2008). *Multicultural Societies: Challenges and Prospects.* Brittan Publishers.

Waterbury, J. (1979). *Introduction to Hydropolitics.* Netherlands Water Institute.

Weber, M. (1968). *Economy and Society: An Outline of Interpretive Sociology.* Volume 1. Penguin Publishers.

Weber, M. (1947). *Theory of Social and Economic Organization.* New York. Free Press.

Wenyang, A. (2022). *China Covid-19 Manufacturing Shock.* Beijing Printers

Williamson, D. (1958). *Taking River Nile in the Hands.* British Water Resources Institute-London

Wimmer, A. (2013). *Ethnic Boundary Making: Institutions, Power and Networks.* Oxford University Press.

World Bank, *Report,* 1997

Wright, G. (2011). Student-Centred Learning in Higher Education. *International Journal of Teaching and Learning in Higher Education.* Vol 23 (3): 92-97

Wright, E and Shin, K. (1988). *Temporality and Class Analysis: A comparative Study of the Effects of Class Trajectory and Class Structure on Class Consciousness in Sweden and United States.* Semantic Scholars.

Wrong, M. (2009). *It's Our Turn to Eat: The Story of a Kenyan Whistle-Blower.* Harper Collins.

Yong, D. (2023). Chinese Post-Covid-19 Myth Economy Recovery. *Shandong Briefs.* Shandong.

Young, J. (1999). *Ethnicity and the Complex World.* Macmillan.

Zeihan, P. (2022). The End of the World is Just the Beginning: Mapping the Collapse of Globalization, Harper Audio.

Zeitoum, M. (2010). *Power, Hegemony and Critical Hydropolitics: Transboundary Water Management, Principles and Practices*. Basic Books.

Zolberg, A. (1998). *The Coup D' Etat in Theory and Practice*. University of Chicago Press.

INDEX

www.ingramcontent.com/pod-product-compliance
Lightning Source LLC
Chambersburg PA
CBHW021857020426

42334CB00013B/368